Sefer Yom LeYom

Day by Day

Written by
Reb Moshe Steinerman

Edited by Elise Teitelbaum

Ilovetorah Jewish Outreach Network

Ilovetorah Jewish Publishing
First Published 2018
ISBN: 978-1-947706-06-4

Editor: Elise Teitelbaum
Co-editor: Rochel Steinerman

ABOUT THE AUTHOR

Rabbi Moshe Steinerman grew up as a religious Jew on the hillsides of Maryland. During his teenage years, Reb Moshe developed his talent for photography, while connecting to nature and speaking to *HaShem*. He later found his path through Breslev *Chassidus*, while maintaining closeness to the *Litvish* style of learning. He studied in the Baltimore yeshiva, Ner Yisrael; then married and moved to Lakewood, New Jersey. After settling down, he began to write *Kavanos Halev*, with the blessing of *Rav* Malkiel Kotler *Shlita*, Rosh Yeshiva of Beis Medresh Gevoha.

After establishing one of the first Jewish outreach websites, IloveTorah.com in 1996, Reb Moshe's teachings became popular among the full spectrum of Jews, from the unaffiliated to ultra-Orthodox. His teachings, including hundreds of stories of tzaddikim, gained popularity due to the ideal of drawing Jews together. Reb Moshe made aliyah to Tzfat in 2003 and since then has been helping English-speaking Jews to return to Judaism through his popular Jewish videos and audio shiurim. His learning experience includes the completion of both Talmud Bavli and Yerushalmi as well as other important works.

In 2012, Reb Moshe, with his wife and children, moved to Jerusalem. Some of his other books are Kavanos Halev (Meditations of the Heart), Tikkun Shechinah, Tovim Meoros (Glimpse of Light), Chassidus, Kabbalah & Meditation, Prayers of the Heart, Pesukei Torah (Passages of Torah), Pathways of the Righteous, A Journey into Holiness, and The True Intentions of the Baal Shem Tov. Thousands have read the advice contained in these books, with life-changing results.

In Memory of my father Shlomo Zavel Ben Yaakov ZT"L
My father-in-law Menachem Ben Reuven ZT"L
And all the great souls of our people

I grew up in a house filled with the Torah learning of my father, who studied most of the day. Although there were no Jews in this remote part of Maryland, my father was a man of chesed to all people and was known for his brilliance in Torah scholarship.

In Memory of My grandparents Yaakov Ben Shmuel Zavel, Toba Esther bas Gedlaya Aharon Hakohein, Yehudah ben Ike, Isabbela Bas Israel My great-grandmother Nechama bas Sara Rivka, My Uncle Shmuel Yosef ben Gedalya Aharon Hakohein

I want to say a special thank you to the Nikolsberg Rebbe and the Biala Rebbe for their encouragement and blessings. Most of all, I offer thanks to my wife, Rochel, for her faithful support.

*Dedicated to my wife Rochel
and to my children Shlomo Nachman, Yaakov Yosef,
Gedalya Aharon Tzvi, Esther Rivka, Yeshiya Michel,
Dovid Shmuel, Eliyahu Yisrael
may it bring forth the light of your neshamos.*

Dear Reader,

Ilovetorah Jewish Outreach is a non-profit and books and Torah classes are available at low costs. Therefore, we appreciate your donation to help Rabbi Moshe Steinerman and ilovetorah.com to continue their work on behalf of the Jewish people. We also ask that you pass on these books to others once you are finished with them.

Thank you,
Reb Moshe Steinerman

RABBINIC APPROVALS / HASKAMAHS

בס״ד

RABBI DOVID B. KAPLAN
RABBI OF WEST NEW YORK
5308 PALISADE AVENUE • WEST NEW YORK, NJ 07093
201-867-6859 • WESTNEWYORKSHUL@GMAIL.COM

דוד ברוך הלוי קאפלאן
רב ואב״ד דק״ק
וועסט ניו יארק

י' שבט ה'תשע"ז / February 6, 2017

Dear Friends,

Shalom and Blessings!

For approximately twenty years I have followed the works of Rabbi Moshe Steinerman, Shlit"a, a pioneer in the use of social media to encourage people and bring them closer to G-d.

Over the years Rabbi Steinerman has produced, and made public at no charge, hundreds of videos sharing his Torah wisdom, his holy stories, and his touching songs. Rabbi Steinerman has written a number of books, all promoting true Jewish Torah spirituality. Rabbi Steinerman's works have touched many thousands of Jews, and even spirituality-seeking non-Jews, from all walks of life and at all points of the globe.

Rabbi Steinerman is a tomim (pure-hearted one) in the most flattering sense of the word.

I give my full approbation and recommendation to all of Rabbi Steinerman's works.

I wish Rabbi Steinerman much success in all his endeavors.

May G-d bless Rabbi Moshe Steinerman, his wife, Rebbetzin Rochel Steinerman, and their beautiful children; and may G-d grant them health, success, and nachas!

With blessings,

Rabbi Dovid B. Kaplan

Appoval of the Biala Rebbe of New York / Betar / Miami

הובא לפני גליונות בעניני קירוב רחוקים לקרב אחינו בני ישראל אל
אביהם שבשמים, כידוע מהבעש"ט זיע"א שאמר "איתמי קאתי מר
לכשיפוצו מעינותיך חוצה" ואפריון נמטי"ה להאי גברא יקירא מיקירי
צפת עיה"ק תובב"א כמע"כ מוהר"ר משה שטיינרמן שליט"א אשר כבר
עוסק רבות בשנים לקרב רחוקים לתורה וליהדות, וכעת מוציא לאור
ספר בשם "יום ליום" וראיתי דברים נחמדים מאוד וניכר מתוך
הדברים שהרב בעל המחבר - אהבת השי"ת ואהבת התורה וישראל
בלבבו, ובטחוני כי הספר יביא תועלת גדולה לכל עם ישראל.

ויה"ר שיזכה לבוא לגומרה ברוב פאר והדר ונזכה לגאולתן של ישראל
בב"א.

בכבוד רב:
אהרן שלמה חיים אליעזר
בלאאאו"ר זצללה"ה אב'יאלא

Rabbi M. Lebovits
Grand Rabbi of
Nikolsburg
53 Decatur Avenue
Spring Valley, N.Y. 10977

יוסף יחיאל מיכל
לעבאוויטש
ניקלשבזרג
מאנסי - ספרינג וואלי, נ.י.

בעזהשי"ת

בשורותי אלו באתי להעיד על מעשה אומן, מופלא מופלג בהפלגת חכמים ונבונים,
ירא וחרד לדבר ה', ומשתוקק לקרב לבית ישראל לאביהם שבשמים,
ה"ה הרב **משה שטיינערמאן** שליט"א בעיה"ק צפת תובב"א

שעלה בידו להעלות על הספר דברים נפלאים שאסף מספרים הקדושים, בענין אהבה
אחוה שלום זריעיות, לראות מעלות חברינו ולא חסרונם, ועי"ז להיות נמנעים מדברי
ריבות ומחלוקת, ולתקן עון שנאת חנם אשר בשביל זה נחרב בית מקדשינו
ותפארתינו, וכמשאחז"ל (רש"י, ויקרא רבה ט' ב') על ויהן שם ישראל, שניתנה תורה באופן
שחנו שם כאיש אחד בלב אחד.

וניכר בספר כי עמל וינע הרבה להוציא מתח"י דבר נאה ומתוקן, ע"כ אף ידי תכון
עמו להוציאו לאור עולם, ויהי רצון שהפיץ ה' בידו יצליח, יברך ה' חילו ופועל ידו
תרצה, שיברך על המוגמר להגדיל ולהאדירה תורה ולהפיצו בקרב ישראל, עד ביאת
גוא"צ בב"א.

א"ד הכותב לכבוד התורה ומרביציה,
י"ט חשון תשס"ו

Rabbi Abraham Y. S. Friedman
161 Maple Avenue #C Spring Valley NY 10977
Tel: 845-425-5043 Fax: 845-425-8045

אברהם יחזקאל שרגא פרידמאן
רב דביהמ"ד אמר"י ספר"ר קאמאדא
וראש כולל האר"י

בעזהשי"ת

ישפות השם החיים והשלו', לכבוד ידידי מאז ומקדם מיקירי קרתא
דירושלים יראה שלם, זוכה ומזכה אחרים, להיות דבוק באלקינו, ה"ה
הר"ר משה שטיינרמאן שליט"א.

שמחתי מאוד לשמוע ממך, מאתר רחוק וקירוב הלבבות, בעסק
תורתך הקדושה ועבודתך בלי לאות, וכה יעזור ה' להלאה ביתר שאת
ויתר עז. והנה שלחת את הספר שלקטת בעניני דביקות בה', לקרב
לבבות בני ישראל לאבינו שבשמים בשפת אנגלית, אבל דא עקא
השפת לא ידענו, ע"כ לא זכיתי לקרותו, ע"א א"א לי ליתן הסכמה פרטי
על ספרך, ובכלל קיבלתי על עצמי שלא ליתן הסכמות, ובפרט כשאין
לי פנאי לקרות הספר מתחלתו עד סופו, אבל בכלליות זכרתי לך חסד
נעוריך, היאך הי' המתיקות שלך בעבדות השם פה בעירינו, ובנועם
המדות, וחזקה על חבר שאינו מוציא מתחת ידו דבר שאינו מתוקן,
ובפרט שכל מגמתך להרבות כבוד שמים, שבוודאי סייעתא דשמיא
ילווך כל ימיך לראות רב נחת מיוצ"ח ומפרי ידיך, שתתקבל הספר
בסבר פנים יפות אצל אחינו בני ישראל שמדברים בשפת האנגלית
שיתקרבו לאבינו שבשמים ולהדבק בו באמת כאות נפשך, ולהרבות
פעלים לתורה ועבודה וקדושה בדביקות עם מדות טובות, בנייחותא
נייחא בעליונים ונייחא בתחתונים עד ביאת גואל צדק בב"א.

כ"ד ידידך השמח בהצלחתך ובעבודתך

[חתימה]

[חתימה]

TABLE OF CONTENTS

Reb Moshe Steinerman

OVERVIEW

With the help of HaShem, I am pleased to complete my fourth work in the writings of Torah. This sefer was written on my online blog throughout the years, as I was spreading the light of Torah to the masses. I started the project while living in the holy city of Tzfat and completed it in the holy city of Jerusalem.

Inspired by the beauty of life's simplicity and covering many aspects of life, Sefer Yom Leyom, is divided into 50 chapters comprised of advice on various topics of life. Some of the teachings and thoughts were purposely not completed, in order that the reader should reach a deep understanding on their own of how the concept mentioned can be applied in his personal life. Other teachings are meant to come right to the point and can hit a person like an arrow to the heart.

King Solomon pointed out, "There is nothing new under the sun (Proverbs)." As much as these are original Torah thoughts, their sources are found in the Torah and Sages. Every concept is, therefore, *emes*, truth, meant to help you find practical answers for your everyday life. Sometimes it takes a simple proverb and concept to enlighten one's path. With this idea, Sefer Yom Leyom has come to fruition.

INTRODUCTION

The soul of a Jew is from the highest levels of purity, its sparks of G-dliness reaching higher than the purest of angels on high. When we comprehend our own strength, then we will connect to the higher levels of our soul's root and perfect our soul as intended. For this reason, we have been created and the test of each of us is to strive for this perfection.

It is the confusions of this world that get the better of us and separate us from our soul root. We are constantly seeking practical advice and words of comfort, to get us through each day. *Yom Leyom*, day by day, we have to take one step at a time, and make a new beginning in our service of HaShem. Without this ideology, we simply can't advance and improve.

The wisdom of our sages is here to guide us, as they have trodden the same paths we are following now, yet they seem to have overcome all the obstacles! So too, we have the inner strength and the Torah's guidance to do the same. Otherwise, HaShem wouldn't face us with our current challenges.

We shouldn't need the rabbis to hold our hands and to think for us, though they are here to guide us. Our souls already are completely attached to the Creator on high. It is just that we are filled with too much confusion to hear the inner messages our soul sends us.

Through humility, we are able to listen to the calls of our soul and to open the channels of *binah*. Each sage with precision has attempted to climb through these fifty gates of *binah*, seeking perfect understanding. Some fell down after a few gates and then persevered, climbing to even greater heights. Others fell and never returned. A few of our great rabbis reached the forty-ninth and fiftieth gates through constant effort and toil, believing they should never give up.

As you move closer to true understanding and *emes*, the battlefield appears more gruesome. Sparks are flying in all directions, some from points of good and others from bad, trying to knock you off course. It takes *chochmah*, to duck these negative sparks and reach the next higher level. Only through the study of Torah will a person gain the wisdom to know right from wrong, truth from falsehood; reach the horizon and make the right choices.

My holy friends, you must persevere and battle the storms that confuse you, that are trying to take you off course. The sages are there to help you, but only you can fight this inner battle between the *yetzer hara* and *yetzer hatov*. It is within your power to knock down each obstacle with grace and courage, like a lion seeking its prey - the prey being complete mastery of your body and soul.

Should you overcome your tests in life, there is an endless reward in this world and the world to come. Even though each of us is faced with different tasks, we are still the same. The ladder might be a different color, but it has the same number of steps on it; steps that may seem slippery at first but are climbable, using the tools given to us by the Torah.

You could take the easy way out and stay on your present level; that is what most people do. They are comfortable with where they are holding in life and some have made peace with their sins, continuing to act upon them daily and thereby ignoring the true meaning of life.

To rise above the status quo and be a light unto the nations, you can never be satisfied with your current state of being. You have to understand where you are truly holding in your *madrega*, level, and yet strive to accomplish much more. The light and purity for HaShem has to thirst within your very bones and sinews. It must do so to such an extent that you're willing to do anything for HaShem, even cast away the pleasures of this world.

Yom Leyom, day by day, you must crave *HaShem* and give all your being to His service. A day that you didn't give one hundred percent is a day lost forever. Not only this, but it will also affect the next day's service and you will feel as if you need to catch up to your previous level, instead of climbing the next step where you truly belong.

Do not worry though; this is to be expected from time to time. We are not angels living in a completely pure world! We are human, and we will fall often. These falls are painful to our souls and sometimes leave us in the state of feeling completely alone. During these periods, may <u>Sefer Yom Leyom</u> be a comfort to you and help you make a fresh start with the *daas*, the understanding from our holy sages. Through this, may you reach completeness of self and bring about rectifications to all mankind. The sages teach us: with proper repentance and change to a pure path in the service of HaShem, even your sins can be turned into merits. Therefore, there is always hope.

FIFTY CHAPTERS OF BINAH,

UNDERSTANDING

CHAPTER 1:
WISDOM

1. A wise person lacks nothing.
2. If you have true wisdom, then you realize how little you really know.
3. Wisedom begins with the love of HaShem.
4. Put your opinions to the side and listen to others, then you will gain true wisdom.
5. The wise read many books, constantly seek more knowledge, and apply it to life.
6. An intelligent person works for their wisdom, and you should respect them for their dedication to this.
7. Wisdom alone, without understanding, isn't enough. Understanding comes from experience.
8. People who are wise in Torah, beyond their years, may have a very pure heart.
9. Think of *YKVK* with the *nikud* of *patach* in order to open (*patach*) your heart. To gain the highest wisdom, think of it with *patach, segol, segol, patach*.
10. Being wise means to know how to fill your soul with new knowledge at the level it can receive, and not seek what is beyond its capabilities.
11. If you're wise, you make decisions and actions with balance.
12. Too much worldly knowledge, without the majority of knowledge from the Torah, leads a person to second-guess HaShem.
13. Doing things such as walking, speaking or eating with a hurried step causes one to lose wisdom.
14. If you have a warehouse full of wisdom and have no way to empty it to others, what purpose does it have?

15. A wise person realizes how valuable time is.
16. Always keep some of your wisdom hidden from the world. If you give it all away, you will feel completely empty.
17. A truly wise person doesn't see others as being beneath them, but rather someone they can learn from.
18. A lazy person doesn't care about gaining wisdom, and their inner world is one of loneliness.

CHAPTER 2:
REPENTANCE

1. If you understood how simple it can be to repent, and be forgiven by HaShem, you would find repentance comes easily. However, Satan wants you to think that you can't really change your ways and be granted forgiveness.

2. Don't say you're going to repent later when you have time, but rather grab the moment right now when your heart is open.

3. A happy heart makes it easier to repent. It is very difficult to ask forgiveness while you're stuck in sadness.

4. Satan wants you to worry and feel heaviness in your soul, even after you repent; it is important not to worry and also to forgive yourself.

5. It is easier to ask HaShem for forgiveness than to harm another human being, who will find it more difficult to be merciful and forgive you.

6. Going to a *tzaddik*, or the grave of a holy sage, is a practical way to open your heart, so your repentance will be accepted.

7. You have to believe in your repentance, that HaShem will grant you complete forgiveness.

8. After repentance comes joy and salvation.

9. Saying the Psalms of King David helps a person acquire an open heart and be forgiven.

10. Going to the *mikvah* as soon as possible following one's sin is very helpful.

11. Saying the ten Psalms of the *tikkun haklali* brings forgiveness.

12. A quiet place with running water and beautiful surroundings helps to open one's heart to repent.

13. Doing *hisbodidus* and talking to Hashem is very redeeming for the soul.

14. Better to try to repent, even if you aren't sincere, than not to try at all. At least there will be a chance, while you're asking forgiveness that your heart will open, and you will begin to truly mean what you say.

15. Call out to HaShem, even in a last effort not to sin. There is always an ability to stop and save yourself, even after you have started to sin.

16. One moment of pure repentance can earn you all the life of the world to come.

17. Constantly dwelling on your faults doesn't lead you to repentance, but rather draws you more to sin.

18. Repentance isn't something complicated. It was created to be very simple. Don't be afraid to repent many times a day if necessary, as the main thing is to have a pure heart for HaShem.

CHAPTER 3:
HEALING

1. A person is healed at the predestined time from Heaven.
2. Giving charity improves your health.
3. A person could be sick because they must increase their fear of HaShem and recognition of Him.
4. Pray for others who are similarly sick, and you will G-d willing, recover more quickly along with them.
5. The *Shechinah* is sick and in pain along with a person who is ill. She remains alongside the bed providing comfort. So why should we pray for our friend when we should be happy the *Shechinah* is there alongside them? Because, should they recover, the *Shechinah* will remain with them, and they will both be elevated together.
6. Medications have healing powers only because of the act of taking them, not for the ingredients. As we know, the wrong medicine can make a person much worse. Only by accepting HaShem as the ultimate Healer does the proper treatment begin to actually work.
7. If you're going to a doctor, at the very least go to the best.
8. Just as the doctor has been given the ability to heal, so too they has been given the power to do damage. Therefore, trust in them only as an agent of HaShem, and nothing more, then they will be given the power to heal you.
9. Some doctors have been blessed with a special connection to healing. They worked very hard for this ability and they are a rare find.

10. If a doctor heals you miraculously, this doesn't mean you should push your friend to use them. It was preordained that you should visit this particular doctor to heal you. Your friend might need a different path to his cure.

11. If you repent daily for your misdeeds and take good care of your health, there are fewer reasons for you to be sick.

12. Should your friend be sick, support them by being there for them.

13. Most people keep a distance from people who are sick and treat them poorly. It is actually these people they should be spending more time with, rather than their healthy friends. This is because HaShem supports the weak and the *Shechinah* is with them. If you are there, in your friend's merit you too can see salvation in your life.

14. If you're not well, call out to HaShem all the more. He is certainly eager to hear your voice or you wouldn't be stricken with this illness.

15. Some people think that sickness weakens a person when it actually makes them stronger.

16. Happiness can heal all the bones.

17. Eating slowly and keeping a good diet is the best medicine.

18. Go to the *tzaddik* and give him a *pidyon*, just in case your illness is worse than you might have thought. Only the *tzaddik* brings about your *tikun* if your soul is very sick.

CHAPTER 4:
SOUL

1. The soul of every Jew is very holy and yearns to be connected to HaShem.

2. Just as you visit a doctor when your body is sick, you should visit the *tzaddik* when your soul feels sick.

3. All your soul expects from you is that you give 100% effort in coming close to HaShem. Obviously, it understands the hardships of this world and how it can distance you.

4. Be careful to immerse in the *mikvah* every three days; your soul will feel security if you do this.

5. It is important to leave a wash basin near your bed at night, as your soul feels pain if it isn't nearby.

6. Attach your soul to a *tzaddik* by concentrating on some *sefirah* they might be connected to, and then imagine that you both are climbing from this place up the *sefiros* to *Binah*, where you will simultaneously be elevated.

7. Mediate, from time to time, that you are binding your soul to the *Shechinah*.

8. All the soul desires is to reattach to the Heavenly worlds, from whence it came.

9. When you do a sin, you are torturing the *Shechinah* along with your soul.

10. No matter how many sins you perform, your soul is still attached to a pureness above. That is why you are able to repent.

11. The study of Torah is the best remedy for the soul, as it attaches to the Torah for cleansing.

12. People underestimate the power of their own soul and how great it truly is.

13. Holy sparks of the sages can attach themselves to every soul that performs *mitzvos* with *kavanah*. These sparks sometimes remain for a few minutes, hours, days, or years.
14. A person's soul needs joy.
15. Depression does severe damage to the soul; sometimes it is very hard to repair such damage.
16. Giving a *pidyon*, visiting the graves of holy sages, or sending someone there on your behalf, can revive your soul.
17. Just as the body needs food and water to survive, so too the soul needs Torah and *mitzvos*.
18. It is beneficial to have your name written on parchment, intertwined with the word *neshamah*.

CHAPTER 5:
NATURE

1. The beauty of nature and a walk through the forest can calm the soul unlike other efforts.
2. Seeing and listening to water has a way of opening one's mind to wisdom and understanding. It can also increase one's memory.
3. It is good for the soul to wander amongst the trees of the forest, to meditate on HaShem and one's personal life.
4. If you're unsure which path to choose, sometimes a river or waterfall can remove confusing thoughts, allowing you to decide the best direction.
5. The beauty in nature can help a person realize that HaShem is in charge of all events, and has created everything with great attention to detail.
6. Sometimes, by taking a walk in a quiet park, a person can really reflect on what is important and institute real changes in his life.
7. Animals have a way of opening up a person's heart that was otherwise closed, due to some hurtful experience.
8. When you see the colors of nature, try to reflect on the *sefirah* connected to each color, thereby elevating the object on high.
9. Animals have a very simple way of life and are constantly singing praises to HaShem. We can learn from this simplicity.
10. If we don't pray to HaShem for our daily needs, we are no different from animals. This is because He gives to each and every living organism its needs, regardless if it asks or not. Therefore, one should specifically pray for their basic necessities daily.

11. A person should respect all creations, since at every moment they are given *shefa* from Above, just as we are. They are similar to a large orchestra playing in unison for the conductor.
12. Don't kill insects and animals unnecessarily.
13. A person whose nature it is to care for an animal in pain will most likely do so for a human being as well.
14. It is important to have plenty of sun and air, as they are agents of HaShem to heal the creations at proper, preordained intervals.
15. At least once or twice a week, a person should leave the city, or find a quiet place to rest their mind, in a more natural environment.
16. Nature can humble a person.
17. It can be depressing to spend too much time in nature and not enough time among human companions.
18. Teach your children to appreciate nature, it will soften their heart.

CHAPTER 6:
LAZINESS

1. If you're going to do something, do it with 100% effort, with all your might and attention. Continue to do everything in life with this method and you will be successful.
2. Too much sleeping and eating makes a person lazy.
3. We have a tendency to pray with laziness. This is because prayer is so powerful that our evil inclination tries to distract us, convincing us how tiring it is to recite the words with thought and intention.
4. If you're around lazy people often, their laziness will be contagious, and pull you in along with them.
5. Stay close to people who value their time and life. It will be good for your soul and rub off on you.
6. It is important while you're young to acquire the character trait of brazenness when it comes to performing the *mitzvos*. How many mitzvos did we miss out on because we were too shy to perform them publicly?
7. If you have any real intelligence, you won't waste your life away with laziness.
8. Should you be unclear if your reservations about doing something are pure or just laziness, open up a Torah book. Study for a moment the passage you come to; the answer often will become clear to you. This is a lower form of *ruach hakodesh*.
9. Just as one *mitzvah* leads to another *mitzvah*, one action leads to another action.
10. Fight laziness with all your heart, as it is something that can lead you to very negative values.

11. Put off your lazy moments by telling yourself you will be lazy in a while from now. When that time comes, put it off again and again, in order to set laziness aside for the day.
12. Depression leads to inertia.
13. Even if you don't generally enjoy some project that has to be done, persevere and do it wholeheartedly, and you will feel good about it.
14. Success will give you far more enjoyment than the few minutes you take for goofing off, which have no lasting benefit and will soon be forgotten.
15. Encourage and teach others not to be lazy and this will effect your soul too, by reminding yourself to do better.
16. When you feel lazy, start something new and positive in your life.
17. When you start something, commit to finishing it.
18. Exercising is a good habit to rid you of laziness.
19. Physical laziness leads to spiritual laziness.
20. Don't ask others to do something for you, that you can do yourself. Become accustomed to being independent.

CHAPTER 7:
THE LAND OF ISRAEL

1. Living or connecting to the Land of Israel is beneficial for overcoming any type of physical desire.
2. The land of Israel draws fear of HaShem into a person's heart.
3. It is possible to connect to the holiness of Israel while outside of her. Your great longing for her can connect you to the soul root of the holy land.
4. Torah study while living in Israel has more fullness and energy to cause your soul to be upright.
5. It is a great *mitzvah* to own land or an apartment in Israel.
6. The more you appreciate the Land of Israel, the more it will embrace you in return to make you a part of it.
7. People tend to spend less money on material things in Israel as the cravings for them are less.
8. It is very beneficial spiritually to live or frequently visit one of the four holy cities, as they contain special holy elements to open the gates of prayer and Torah: Jerusalem, Tzfat, Tiberias, and Chebron.
9. Try to visit Israel with the intention of self-growth and renewal of ideals. Don't return home just to continue in the same way as before.
10. Living in Israel brings a person greater responsibility to behave in a holier way.
11. A person who lives outside of Israel with the intention to spread the light of Torah, to those far from HaShem, has a special portion in the holy land.
12. The lands outside of Israel are filled with emptiness.

13. Just as prayer in Jerusalem has much more power than most prayers said elsewhere, Torah study in Jerusalem also has the remarkable strength to purify.
14. Helping people who live in Israel gives you a portion with them in the land.
15. A person should always strive to come to Israel, physically or even just spiritually, in his thoughts.
16. Since a person is wherever his thoughts are, place your thoughts in the holiness of Israel and allow her to cleanse you.
17. If you live in Israel, then you must strive to appreciate this blessing every day. It is a great merit to be invited by HaShem to be here and to remain. There were many holier than yourself who didn't have this opportunity.
18. It is possible to live in Israel, but have your heart living elsewhere. Keep both your body, and soul, in the holy land.

CHAPTER 8:
MOSHIACH

1.   The *moshiach* will come as soon as people at least try to care about getting along with one another, but this simple step seems a huge mountain to overcome.

2.   Can you imagine that you're in a marathon and thousands of people are waiting for you to reach the finish line, but you're running the wrong way or leisurely enjoying breaks along the way? Our relatives are watching above, wondering why we don't repent and do more *mitzvos* so that the redemption will come immediately.

3.   If people really wanted the *moshiach* to come, he would be here.

4.   Don't you want to leave this world knowing you did everything you could to usher in the redemption for your descendants?

5.   All of us worry about our children. We care for them with all of our hearts, but we should provide for our families, not only with material life insurance, but also with an everlasting peace that will hasten the *moshiach*, even after we have left this world.

6.   If people would realize the power that even one Jewish soul has to bring the final redemption! There is no such thing as just an ordinary Jewish soul.

7.   The *moshiach's* arrival is more imminent than we realize. We can feel him so close, but the last waiting period feels the longest.

8.   Hasten the *moshiach's* arrival with an increase in the performance of good deeds for others.

9.   Through studying about the messianic times, you become part of the redemption itself.

10. Torah study with the intention of true change and actual practice is what draws the *moshiach* closer.

11. A person of true faith has to believe in the *moshiach*.

12. As my father *zt"l* used to say, "Does it matter if the *moshiach* comes on a Friday or a *shabbos*? If he comes first from the north or the south? Let him just come anywhere and anytime."

13. Like most things in *Yiddishkeit*, it is best to take the middle path when it comes to the *moshiach*. Believe in his imminent arrival, prepare yourself with the learning of *karbonos* and the laws of messianic times, yet try to give over messianic teachings to others gently, without force.

14. Telling over stories and Torah teachings from the messianic times inspire a person to have faith.

15. If you want to bring the *moshiach*, remove all hate from your heart.

16. The study of Torah at midnight and the recital of *tikkun chatzos* are the best *tikunim* a person can do to usher in the messianic times.

17. If someone you know is reciting *tikkun chatzos* and studying Torah at midnight, know that this person has a portion in the final redemption. Do everything you can to help them. Even if it means through charity, picking up their kids at daycare, or bringing them meals.

18. Those who arise for *chatzos*, to do *avodas* HaShem, have a special power to bless others, as they are connected to the roots of *shefa* and the *moshiach* himself.

CHAPTER 9:
WORLDLY PLEASURES

1. Material things provide a person with only temporary enjoyment.
2. If you don't look at something, you won't have a desire for it.
3. Too much craving of worldly things leads to depression or sin.
4. Worldly pleasures are usually soon forgotten, whereas holy pleasures are recalled and cherished forever.
5. People think that material things will fix their problems but, most often, they don't.
6. Once you buy something materialistic you will wish for an upgrade, to something better, because there is no quenching the thirst for *gashmius*. You will only crave more and more.
7. Unless you really need something, don't buy it.
8. Try not to get lost in desires; it's hard to find your way back from them.
9. Be happy in HaShem and your family, not in your possessions.
10. Many times material items just end up broken, unused as originally intended or left in a storage box, as they don't provide pleasure as first thought.
11. Vacations are not always as pleasant as planned. This is because they usually cost more than originally calculated. The living arrangements are noisy or not comfortable, and you get lost in unfamiliar surroundings. Travel is very tiring and unexpected things happen to ruin your vacation.
12. Worldly pleasures are there to distract us from the study of Torah.

13. It is bad enough that you crave worldly things, don't encourage friends to do so as well.
14. This world is only temporary, and you can't take worldly possessions with you.
15. The more worldly things you possess and get involved with, the less time you have to meditate and think about what's really important.
16. If you can't stop thinking about the desire for some worldly pleasure, chances are that, once you pursue it, this thing will also drive you away from HaShem.
17. If you can't share some worldly pleasure with another person who will benefit as much as you, what good is it?
18. Life is too short to worry about pleasures that will not be everlasting in the world to come.

CHAPTER 10
MIRACLES AND SALVATION

1. Miracles happen when you least expect them.
2. When you appreciate all the miracles that have already happened to you, then you might be blessed with a new one.
3. Don't put yourself in a position where you have to rely upon a miracle to survive.
4. HaShem doesn't like to do open miracles very often, so pray for a hidden one, or for Him to help you through natural means.
5. We don't thank HaShem enough for the miracles that have already happened to us.
6. People who are suffering sometimes need just a little more patience. Many times salvation is already on its way, but it has to happen at the time ordained for it.
7. If you want salvation, say the Psalms; they open all of the doors for a blessing.
8. Happiness and positive thinking lead to salvation and relief.
9. Faith leads to miracles and salvation.
10. When the time of salvation is near, changes happen very quickly.
11. Before something wonderful is going to happen to you, something bad (in your eyes) may need precede it.
12. A *tzaddik* has the power to bring about unplanned miracles.
13. Immersion in the *mivkah* brings salvation and relief.
14. When you repent completely, miracles can happen openly for you.

15. HaShem is not going to trouble Himself to perform a miracle for someone who won't even recognize or appreciate it.
16. Torah study leads to salvation when done *lishmah*, for the sake of the *mitzvah* itself.
17. If salvation comes after a long time, it is more appreciated.
18. When you're faced with a big test from your evil inclination, and you choose to forego the pleasures of this world, you open up the channels for salvation.

CHAPTER 11
PEACE

1. If you don't have inner peace, how can you make peace with the world and its inhabitants?
2. When you pursue a peaceful relationship with others, you find peace in your own heart.
3. When you don't owe others money, you feel at peace.
4. The most important peace is with your family.
5. Sometimes it is worth losing money to avoid an argument.
6. Peace doesn't mean you have to let everyone take advantage of you.
7. The *Shechinah* slips away from places that are filled with anger, rage, and hate.
8. Sometimes peace can be bought; however, that may not be a true peace that lasts.
9. Giving charity blesses you with peace in your life.
10. Run far away from situations that might lead you to controversy.
11. There are peaceful ways of dealing with most situations.
12. Stay away from people who are always getting into conflicts.
13. When you dwell on a situation, it becomes heavier than if you chose to ignore it.
14. If you increase your time studying Torah, peace will also increase in your life.
15. Should you not judge against others, you will find peace with yourself and your neighbors.
16. Joy leads to peace.
17. When you respect, or love someone, you try harder to make peace with them.

18. Should you try and find it impossible to make peace with someone, ask others to intervene on your behalf; perhaps they can find a way.

CHAPTER 12:
GRACE

1.   A *segulah* for grace is to study Torah while standing up.
2.   If you do things hurriedly, you don't always do them gracefully.
3.   Being careful to be clean helps a person to become graceful.
4.   Connecting to the *tzaddik* helps a person to bring grace to his life.
5.   If you are nervous, you will make mistakes and not act gracefully.
6.   Happiness leads to doing things with grace.
7.   If you over-think something, you can cause the outcome to end ungracefully.
8.   *Daas* helps a person to perform acts with grace.
9.   Graceful people are often blessed with many friends. People want to be around someone who thinks before they act.
10. When the *Shechinah* is with you, everything you do is with grace.
11. Just because something happens gracefully, doesn't always mean the outcome will be successful.
12. If you do things out of panic and desperation, the outcome will surely not be one of grace.
13. Exercising helps a person to do things gracefully.
14. Prayer leads a person to act graceful in all things.
15. The Torah is grace.
16. Realizing that everything comes from HaShem helps a person to live gracefully and happily.
17. Good smells and confidence help a person to be graceful.
18. Immersion in the *mikvah* leads to gracefulness.

CHAPTER 13:
MARRIAGE

1. It takes two humble people to make a marriage successful.
2. Marriage is about giving to another and then having children to give to together.
3. If you don't have peace with yourself it is difficult to have with another, especially a spouse who sees all your flaws and mistakes.
4. Love that comes quickly is flawed. One that builds over time is strong and real.
5. In marriage you will be forced many times to put aside some of your goals in order to make your spouse happy. In that process, another one's desires might need to come before your own.
6. Being a step ahead of your spouse's needs goes a long way to providing a healthy home.
7. If there is no peace in the home, children grow up with many confusions and anger.
8. One pushes away their spouse, when they need them the most, because they feel they aren't cared for. This creates a chain reaction, where the other half may reciprocate with indifference. Don't continue on this vicious cycle, communicate your feelings with each other.
9. The holiness of one spouse effects the other over time.
10. Sometimes in marriage you have to do a lot of acting and pretending, so the other partner doesn't feel your sorrow and anger.

11. A depressed partner brings heaviness to their spouse and children.

12. Your spouse may not always appreciate your actions, so sometimes you need to find their appreciation within yourself, and just carry on. HaShem sees all of your good deeds, and His appreciation for your selflessness is even more important.

13. Don't go to sleep or leave your home with anger.

14. Being able to say you're sorry, even if you don't mean it yet, is the start to a meaningful relationship.

15. When you realize that your spouse's anxiety and pains are your own, then you can both heal together.

16. It is important to eat meals together, and to go out of the house together, so that you feel like one unit in private and in public.

17. Never threaten your spouse with separation or divorce unless you are serious. The pain you cause through this threat can be far worse than the pain you yourself feel now.

18. Do not discuss your marriage with family members; it is impossible for them to be impartial and you cause an everlasting friction between your spouse and your family.

CHAPTER 14:
MEMORY

1. The Torah learning that you accidentally forget should not worry you too much, as it will be reminded to you in the next world.
2. A person's brain can retain more and more information when it is pure.
3. Olive oil is a *segulah* for improving memory.
4. If you're humble, your memory improves and can store endless amounts of information.
5. The secular wisdom that is of no real use clogs one's memory and thoughts of purity.
6. A healthy diet keeps your memory and mind become clear.
7. Stress and anxiety lead to forgetfulness.
8. The more Torah you study, the greater your memory will be.
9. Worry leads to forgetfulness.
10. Eating with *kavanah*, reciting the blessings before and after meals with proper intentions, leads to a vibrant memory.
11. Exercise helps a person to acquire a good memory and positive thoughts.
12. Forgetting is not always a bad thing. It can help a person to put the past behind them, so as not to be haunted by their mistakes.
13. It is important to always remember the *tefillin* you are wearing and not forget you have them on.
14. Closeness to *tzaddikim* restores your memory.
15. If you can't remember things, and you start to write them down regularly, eventually it will help you to

retrain your memory. Over time you will see that you will need to rely on these notes less and less. to

16. A person whose life, possessions and schedule are organized has an easier time remembering things.
17. A quiet place has the ability to help a person remember.
18. If you utilize your memory often to perform difficult memory baring tasks, you increase your ability to retain information.

CHAPTER 15:
SUCCESS

1.   Your friend's success should feel like your own.
2.   A person is successful when other people study his original Torah insights.
3.   Until a person has children the age of *chinuch*, he doesn't really have a successful life. Teaching one's children and passing on the tradition of *Yiddishkeit* is what true completion of the soul is about.
4.   A non-Jew judges their success on the material things they have accumulated, and the honors they received. A Jew looks at what *sefarim* they have completed, and their family's portion in Torah and observance.
5.   You can judge your success by the people you know and keep company with. Of course, that should be people who have their priorities in order, who put their Torah values foremost in their life.
6.   Only you and HaShem know your real attainments and merits.
7.   The greatest success comes when you have brought people back to HaShem so they perform many commandments, which are likened to your own merits.
8.   When you care more about the *Shechinah,* and Her success than yours, then you know you have reached a pure level.
9.   If you're worried only about serving HaShem, and less about yourself, HaShem will take care of your life so that everything you do will be completed with grace and success.
10. Many people rely on a successful person for his financial or spiritual support.

11. The more successful you are, the more responsibilities you have.
12. You can't be so successful if you haven't yet reached *yiras* HaShem.
13. You're limiting your achievements when you feel pride, after accomplishing something successfully.
14. Some people become depressed even after they achieve success; this is because their reasons were not pure when performing the *mitzvos* and tasks.
15. If you give charity while performing a chore, then it will help facilitate success.
16. What is successful to one person may not be considered success to someone else. Therefore, don't judge yourself based on other people's opinions, but base them upon your own goals and level.
17. If you attained many things, but you still don't know how to love others, you have attained nothing.
18. Share your success with others; otherwise, you truly can't enjoy it.

CHAPTER 16:
EVIL THOUGHTS

1. Evil thoughts come from food eaten without a proper blessing, or when the standard of *kashrus* is questionable.
2. If you have an improper thought, the best thing is to not pay attention to it, and quickly to think of something else.
3. You might be receiving this wrongful thought in order to remove, and elevate it, from the improper husks. The bad thought might not even come from the source of your soul, so just cast it off and thereby elevate it.
4. If we didn't have an occasional bad thought, we wouldn't appreciate the good thoughts we also have.
5. A person who fears their thoughts lacks self-confidence.
6. Dwelling on an improper thought is like performing it. Ushering it away is synonymous to performing a good deed.
7. A person who is happy doesn't incorporate the evil thoughts that pursue him, so he barely notices them, and they are instantly elevated.
8. When faced with improper thoughts, that you can't seem to get rid of, perform a positive commandment and soon it will go away.
9. HaShem might give us evil thoughts to test us, but He also gives us good thoughts to overcome them.
10. Saying *shema* and *tehillim* are great antidotes for confusing thoughts.
11. Thinking about fear of HaShem removes evil thoughts.

12. Evil thoughts and intentions are brought to a sage while he is praying in order for him to elevate and remove them from the souls of others.

13. If you allow yourself to see something improper, it leads to evil thoughts later that day.

14. The sage who is near you doesn't see the actual bad thought that you have; he just feels your soul slipping from *kedusha*. Fear not, for it is better to be in his presence, where he can help you, than to be alone to fight it off by yourself.

15. Anxiety leads to external thoughts attacking you endlessly.

16. If you switch locations, you might find the evil thoughts going away just from this simple action.

17. Should you surround yourself with holy people, you will find yourself with fewer negative thoughts. Should you find these thoughts increasing instead, it is a sign that the evil inclination is afraid that you will soon overcome it. Therefore, pay no attention to it.

18. Keeping *shabbos* and *yom tov* properly removes negative thoughts.

CHAPTER 17:
SECLUSION

1. With practice, you can seclude yourself with HaShem, even in a situation where you are surrounded by groups of people.
2. Going to the forest helps a person to seclude himself and his thoughts with HaShem.
3. It is important to seclude oneself with HaShem every day, in a place where nobody else is around, and it is quiet.
4. Doing *hisbodedus* and meditation is the best form of seclusion with HaShem.
5. Too much seclusion isn't healthy for a person.
6. Seclusion practiced with extremes can lead to depression and anxiety.
7. When you seclude yourself, do not separate yourself in your mind from the community of Israel. If your intentions are pure, you can bind yourself to others and help their souls along with yours.
8. Your personal connection to HaShem should be your main pursuit; it should be more important to you than your friendships.
9. There are many levels of seclusion. Even staying away from politics, news, shopping and unnecessary gatherings is a form of seclusion with HaShem.
10. To be close to HaShem, you have to sometimes give up friendships. Also, you must stay away from gatherings that you know will lead you to sin or to waste your precious time.
11. *Shabbos* and *yom tov* are the best times to reap the benefits of seclusion.

12. The *yetzer hara* doesn't want you to seclude yourself with HaShem because the benefits thereby to your soul are unfathomable.

13. Practicing deep breathing, from the diaphragm, can help you clear your mind from confusions that keep you away from HaShem.

14. Placing your body in positions that close up the senses is beneficial for the seclusion of the soul. For instance, crossing your arms against your body closes physical senses. Closing your fists, eyes, mouth or folding your legs are other forms of separating yourself from the world.

15. *Tefillin*, if worn properly, helps a person connect to HaShem with all his mind and heart.

16. When your body is clean (through showering or, better yet, the *mikvah*) it is easier to connect to your soul.

17. The prophets first played music, and increased their joy, before pursuing meditation and seclusion. This is because joy helps to elevate the soul.

18. When you tense up all of your muscles and then release them with a deep breath, you remove anxiety and confusions, thereby simplifying your thoughts, and enabling you to seclude yourself with HaShem.

CHAPTER 18:
SWEETENING JUDGMENT

1. Meditation on *YKVK* in white letters with the *nikud* of *segol* sweetens judgment.
2. Immersing in the *mikvah,* and staying under the water a long time, breaks evil decrees.
3. Appreciating what you already have, and being happy with what HaShem has given you, sweetens judgment.
4. Giving charity removes harsh decrees and brings you peace with your fellow man.
5. Saying the Psalms is very valuable for sweetening judgment. It is best to say them after *chatzos* or during the daytime.
6. The *Tikkun Haklali* is a great *tikkun* for the soul, and removes the heaviness that sins place on your body.
7. Dancing removes harsh decrees, elevating the *sefiros* of *Netzach* and *Hod,* to *Binah.*
8. Eating your meals at the table fights all decrees written against you and *Klal Yisrael.*
9. Singing pure *nigunim* sweetens judgment and connects you to the *Shechinah.*
10. Going to the synagogue, to be in HaShem's presence, removes decrees.
11. Prayer at the holy graves of *tzaddikim* removes judgment from your soul.
12. Doing kindness for others can save your soul.
13. When you are faced with sin, but turn away from it, you earn a second chance and any current judgments against you are sweetened.

14. Making a new beginning throughout the day, after you fall down spiritually, sweetens judgment and leads to repentance.

15. A person can commit many sins, but until they speak *loshon hara* against another Jew, they are able to slip under the radar of judgment. This can continue until they eventually repent on their own. However, the second they speak *loshon hara*, they are judged that evening.

16. If you make sure to be at peace with others, you will also have peace in Heaven. Always seek compromises and peace.

17. When you harbor anger, you increase judgments against you.

18. Waking up at midnight to pray and study Torah removes ALL judgments against our nation, as well as your own soul.

CHAPTER 19:
TRAVELING

1. The world is a dangerous place both physically and spiritually. Every time you leave your home, you are a traveler who needs the *Shechinah* to protect you.
2. Traveling with others eases the pain of the journey.
3. Don't travel excessively if it's not necessary. The main place for a person is in the *bais midrash*, or at home with his family.
4. Traveling a long way to see the *tzaddik* is beneficial for the soul.
5. When visiting the graves of our sages, try to keep your journey simple; you will gain the most by concentrating on one particular *rav*.
6. If you travel with a friend, but do not speak on matters of Torah, it would have been better if you traveled alone.
7. It is important when embarking on your journey to be in a state of *shalom* with your family.
8. Should you feel extremely worried about your journey, it might be best to put it off for another time.
9. If you see that you are forced to travel somewhere, HaShem is leading you in to exile, and hoping you will use this time to repent.
10. It is easier to sin while apart from your normal surroundings.
11. Always make sure to eat and drink well during a journey, since traveling weakens the body.
12. You should be extra careful that your eyes don't look at improper things while traveling. Therefore, keep yourself busy with a book or do something productive.

13. You usually spend more money than originally planned during a journey.
14. If you're not sure whether you should go somewhere or not, open up a *sefer* first and read its message. Possibly then you will know if it's right for you to leave.
15. Allowing others to share in a *mitzvah* is a good reason to travel, but leaving early is usually just as important.
16. Always make arrangements, and a proper schedule of your trip, before you set out on any journey.
17. A person who doesn't have to travel so much should be very thankful.
18. The amount of time you waste traveling, and the recovery time for fatigue from your trip, should make you think twice about going on long excursions.

CHAPTER 20:
MODESTY

1. When a person is modest, he has fear of HaShem.
2. If being modest is difficult for you, try to rid yourself of pride.
3. Modesty will save you from friends who wouldn't have been of benefit to your soul.
4. If you are modest, you make fewer mistakes.
5. Don't be afraid to dress modestly; you shouldn't concern yourself with other people's options if your intentions are upright.
6. Be modest, but don't draw special attention to yourself. You should be humble about being modest; otherwise, it may not be genuine.
7. Don't judge another person solely on his mode of dress.
8. A person's modesty can save them from troubles.
9. Be modest in the way you talk to others.
10. A quiet voice is modest and humble.
11. Talk less about yourself and listen more to others.
12. Some colors are more modest than others.
13. Don't jump too quickly to wear extremely modest clothing, if you're not yet ready.
14. You can fool others, but you can't fool HaShem, with a false level of modesty.
15. If your inside isn't like your outside, this can draw more impurity than just being yourself. However, making a change on the outside will eventually effect the inside.
16. There is no real excuse for dressing immodestly. Not only does it effect you, but it also compromises the thoughts of others.

17. Being on top of the latest fashions isn't a modest way to live.

18. Try to dress and act modestly in your home, when only HaShem is watching you, then you can grow both inside and out.

CHAPTER 21:
WEALTH OR POVERTY

1. Appreciate what you have, then you will see that you're wealthier than you had realized.
2. When you're thankful for what you have, HaShem will grant you benevolence.
3. Sometimes having money really isn't the answer. It will only draw you away from holiness.
4. Give charity and you will become wealthy.
5. People who share what they have don't seem to ever be lacking.
6. HaShem listens to the voice of the poor; their prayers have a certain sincerity that the wealthy might have trouble finding.
7. You should be as scared of riches as of poverty.
8. You can't take any of your wealth with you, and when you leave it behind it will most likely be mismanaged. Therefore you should ask yourself, "Why am I so worried about something so temporary?"
9. People fight about money more than other things.
10. A wealthy person is more frightened than a poor person, because the poor person's situation can only improve, while the rich one has to worry that they will have less.
11. A Jew doesn't have to worry much about their sustenance, if they have faith in HaShem.
12. The greatest wealth is one's family.
13. Desire a wealth of knowledge rather than a pocketful of coins.

14. If you are stuck in depression, all the money in the world will only help you temporarily. You must fix the root of your sadness.
15. Your situation will change, as the world is always changing.
16. When you go to work don't leave the study of Torah completely, since chances are you won't return to your learning. Rather schedule your day to accommodate both, according to your needs.
17. If there is a lack of money, there is a lack of peace in the home.
18. Divide your money wisely and never use it all up in one investment.

CHAPTER 22:
A PERSON'S HOME

1. Having a home makes a person feel secure.
2. It is important to take care of one's dwelling and not let it fall apart.
3. The cleaner a person's home is kept, the more clear his thoughts have clarity.
4. Check your *mezuzos* more often than required.
5. The blessing in a person's home comes from the women.
6. Don't acquire a home that you can't afford; it will never really feel like yours when you feel the weight of bills on your shoulders.
7. Make sure that your home is near the *mikvah* and synagogue that you wish to pray in.
8. Be sure that the home you want to buy, or rent, will not require constant upkeep.
9. It only takes one difficult neighbor to make your life stressful.
10. Never trust your landlord or tenant; when it comes to money, people can change at the last moment.
11. Lighting olive oil returns the *Shechinah* into your home.
12. It is important not to compromise when it comes to windows that bring in air and light.
13. Hosting *simchas* in your home, for your family and others, brings down blessings.
14. Owning a home in *Eretz Yisrael* brings a person closer to *Olom Habah*.
15. Make sure your home is filled with practical items, rather than materialistic items.

16. Make sure the Torah is studied every night in your home.
17. It's important to study Torah at home, besides going out to the *bais midrash*, so that your wife and family can feel the sanctity of your learning.
18. If there is fighting in your home, the Satan dwells with you. Through humility, peace will be restored, and your home will be filled with light again.

CHAPTER 23:
HOSPITALITY

1.   A person never forgets those who were hospitable to them.
2.   Many guests lead to a prolonged life.
3.   It is very good, for self-growth, to care for another. Don't let someone enter your home without offering him some hospitality, even a simple drink of water.
4.   When you have a guest, be sure to serve your best food and drinks. HaShem will return it to you in other ways.
5.   If HaShem sees that you care for others enough to invite them into your home, even when you don't have enough for yourself, how can He not be forced to provide more?
6.   Being hospitable can also mean sharing simple things, such as one's seat on the bus, a phone, pen or any item of value to another.
7.   Guests, usher the *Shechinah* into your home.
8.   Having guests removes sadness from your household.
9.   Having guests stay too long at your home can bring confusion to members of your house. It is good to have guests, but not to let them overstay their welcome.
10. Don't have so many guests if it will cause you *shalom bayis* issues.
11. It is one thing to allow someone to stay at your home, but it is a greater challenge to make him so comfortable that he feels at home.
12. A person who is staying at someone's home sometimes feels ashamed to ask for their needs. Therefore, try to be a step ahead of them, and prepare the items they might be too embarrassed to ask for.

13. Try to treat your guests on the level they are accustomed to.

14. Don't leave your guest alone too much; the hardships of traveling can be overcome by the comfort of a friend.

15. Many times, people leave their guests sitting alone in the middle of a *shabbos* meal, while they attend to the children and the food. It is best that at least one family member stays with the guest to engage in conversation; otherwise, it is a bit insulting.

16. When your guest is there, be sure to talk with them about subjects they enjoys, trying to bring HaShem and Torah into the conversation.

17. A person of wisdom can speak about even trivial matters while drawing into the conversation words of wisdom from HaShem.

18. Having guests is a *segulah* for having children.

19. Try not to make your guests feel that they are a burden to you.

CHAPTER 24:
TRUTH

1. If you have to think twice, whether something is truthful or not, then it probably isn't.
2. Truth is one hundred percent truth. Ninety percent truth is mixed with falsehood and is therefore no longer true.
3. Binding to the *tzaddik* helps you to want to become truthful.
4. It is important to be truthful because it helps you acknowledge HaShem's Oneness.
5. Most of the world is filled with falseness and people making believe they are truthful.
6. You can't become a truthful person overnight. You have to work on it for a long time and build a solid foundation of honesty.
7. If you're around many truthful people, the character trait will rub off on you, and vice versa.
8. Inner honesty comes before you can be truthful to others.
9. You will find many times during your lifetime that you are left with a choice, to either take money, or be truthful and miss the opportunity for now. This could even be for a simple task, like paying for the *mikvah* when the door was left open.
10. HaShem takes care of honest people until their very last day.
11. People who are trustworthy are easily recognizable by the way they speak
12. If you are truthful, your children will also follow this path.

13. Involvement in politics confuses a person, so that he can't differentiate between truth and falseness.
14. If you're involved in the *midda* of trustworthiness, you require much less materialism than those who are not.
15. Sometimes our emotions can mask the real truth.
16. If you want to know if something is true, open up a *sefer* and study Torah. Afterwards, meditate on the subject, and you will know if it's from the side of holiness or impurity.
17. If you're confused, ask the *tzaddik* for guidance His connection to the truth will steer you in the correct direction that can sometimes take years to manifest..
18. *Tikkun habris* leads a person to ways of truth.

CHAPTER 25:
TORAH STUDY

1. The greatest way to spend one's time is through Torah study. If you're bored, just study Torah, as it will soothe your soul far more than extracurricular activities.

2. The temptation to stop learning Torah because of life's responsibilities will certainly appear. However, worldly concerns have a way of working out when you study Torah.

3. When you earn your sustenance through your own hands, and then learn Torah, it is far better than living off of others.

4. Always make sure to enjoy what you're learning. Information retained with joy stays with you much longer.

5. Torah study is the best medicine for anxiety and stress.

6. If you want to study Torah, you have to not let anything get in your way.

7. The key to understanding Torah is to study it in order to give it over to others.

8. Teach yourself how to meditate on the Torah that you learn, as the *pasuk* says, "Meditate on the Torah day and night." (Psalms 1:2) Therefore, turn your study into meditations.

9. People always jump ahead of their level in Torah study. Doing this a little is okay, but one should mainly learn at the level they are at presently, so they can slowly build a solid Torah foundation.

10. First, study all of Tanach, then Mishna, then Talmud, and only then Kabbalah. Always learn *mussar* or *chassidus*

alongside your regular study; it will increase your desire to service HaShem.

11. It is very important to learn Ayin Yaakov because the stories of the Talmud will stay with you wherever you go.

12. Torah study without any *halachic* study is a very naive way to serve HaShem.

13. Try to start at the beginning and make sure to finish the Torah books that you began.

14. Learning all books of the Torah slowly doesn't build up your Torah knowledge as well as studying more quickly, and then reviewing the books multiple times.

15. Make sure to learn every *sefer* three times in the course of a few years. When you do this, it is as if you took part in writing it.

16. It is important to study in a *bais midrash*, but also at home because this brings sanctity to your family.

17. Connect yourself to the sages, as you read over their sayings. Bind yourself to their soul roots, by understanding as much as possible.

18. Torah study and prayer go hand in hand. Increase them together, and they will both work for your benefit.

CHAPTER 26:
SAGES / TZADDIKIM

1. HaShem gives us sages to guide us through all of our troubles, but yet we are afraid to approach or bother them. When HaShem said that He gave us the *yetzer hara* and then the antidote, He meant the *tzaddikim*. We can't afford to be scared of them.
2. When we come to the *tzaddikim*, we are helping them too, with our presence and support.
3. The sages are attached to both worlds. When we visit the *tzaddik*, we get a taste of the World to Come.
4. If you can't seem to come close to a *tzaddik*, come close to his students. They will open channels to the sage, so you can draw closer to him.
5. Don't underestimate the blessing of the *tzaddik*, and be sure to have faith in his blessing.
6. Every Jew has the spark of a *tzaddik* inside of them, he merely has to bring it out.
7. The sage has the ability to draw down blessing to Israel. It is very difficult to channel this blessing directly to a person when there might be many obstacles in the way.
8. If you can't study Torah, support a sage who can.
9. Just being in the presence of a sage is enough, even if you haven't the ability to talk with him.
10. If a holy rabbi knows that you won't listen to him, he might feel it's better to tell you less.
11. People often underestimate the sages who are near to them, constantly searching elsewhere when the answers they are seeking are close by.
12. The followers of the sage give him energy to fix the world.

13. It is important to pray with the sage, as you not only help your own soul, but are also assisting him to open the gates of Heaven for all of Israel.

14. Love the sage unconditionally. Many times you will find yourself disappointed since you can't understand him from your vantage point. Judging the sage, pushes away the *Shechinah*.

15. Pray to HaShem that you meet the *tzaddik* who is perfect for you.

16. People often lack respect for a sage who is not their personal rabbi, but this is not correct; he too should be revered.

17. Try to find sages who aren't so involved in political matters. Their involvement might confuse you and cause you to miss the importance of simple Torah observance.

18. Spreading the teachings of your rabbi draws you closer to his soul root. Thereby, you will gain significantly from this.

CHAPTER 27:
YOM TOV

1. The joy that one observes on *yom tov* with, brings him fulfillment for months to come

2. By observing *yom tov* we acquire *emunah*.

3. The more you prepare with excitement for *yom tov*, the more *d'vekus* to HaShem you feel during the holiday.

4. When *moshiach* comes, every day will feel like *shabbos* and *yom tov*.

5. The study of Torah on a *yom tov* is worth many days of normal study.

6. Closeness to family during *yom tov* brings extra blessing to everyone's festival.

7. Glorify your *yom tov* with extra food and the tastiest dishes. Go beyond normal expectations and be glamorous.

8. If the children relate to *yom tov* with presents, then buy them something special.

9. Should you hold back unnecessarily in your observance, and preparation for *yom tov*, so too will HaShem hold back some of the light you were otherwise entitled to.

10. The glory of HaShem can be seen during *yomim tovim*.

11. The wise are able to see the same holy light during *chol hamoed* as they see during *yom tov* itself.

12. Don't get lost in traveling and road trips during *chol hamoed*, all the while losing precious time for a higher level of prayer and Torah study.

13. If you find yourself sad during *yom tov*, you haven't cleared yourself from all of your sins. HaShem desires your repentance so He can shine more light upon you.

14. During *chol hamoed* be careful to work only if absolutely necessary, and even then be careful to connect your heart to *yom tov*, rather than business.

15. If you have a choice, make preparations for *yom tov* yourself, even if it means mopping or other tedious chores. You will get all the time back.

16. Think only joyful and holy thoughts during *yom tov*.

17. Following *yom tov*, you might feel a strong pressure to sin or be depressed. This is because you weren't joyful enough during the holiday.

18. If you open your home to others for *yom tov*, HaShem will open up His storehouses of blessing and holiness, in return.

CHAPTER 28:
SLEEP

1. The purer your soul becomes, the less sleep you require.
2. If you go to sleep with the intention only to refresh your ability to serve HaShem, your sleep becomes a *mitzvah*.
3. Most people sleep either too much or too little.
4. Anxiety and restlessness before sleep is a sign. It means HaShem cares about you and wants you to retire pure after a short confession to Him. A pure soul that is clean has no worries.
5. The main reason people think too much during bedtime is because their soul is warning them to change, and speak more to HaShem.
6. Have you stolen the sleep of others? Maybe this is why you have your own insomnia.
7. When you go to sleep, don't worry so much about tomorrow. Have faith that HaShem, Who doesn't slumber and will be working all night to fix your world.
8. Don't eat or drink too much before sleep.
9. Learn to take deeper breaths, and to breathe from your diaphragm, instead of your chest. Practice this before sleep, until your body learns to relax. This will help the soul to absorb the light from HaShem, at all times.
10. Technology and sleep are opposites.
11. A person who says all of the nighttime prayers has few worries in his life.
12. Always make peace with others before you retire for the evening, and even more so with yourself.
13. HaShem gave sleep to save us from the temptations of the night.

14. Every night, think how blessed you are, You will go to bed happily, looking forward to the next day.
15. When you're doing things you enjoy, you need less sleep, so learn to enjoy everything you do.
16. Clean clothes, sheets, and a clean room help you to fall asleep more easily.
17. Fall asleep on your left side, as the Talmud teaches, and your body's warmth will encourage sleep. If you wake up tossing and turning, switch to your right side.
18. If your soul knows that there is a cup of water to wash your hands with, besides you (preferably covered) for when you awake, it will feel at ease and you will fall asleep peacefully.

CHAPTER 29:
WORK

1. HaShem has *rachmanus*, and opens the gates of prayer, for someone who does his best.
2. The honest man makes more in the long run than one who takes shortcuts, at the expense of others.
3. One should not inflate his ego over his business accomplishments, for without HaShem's original plan, all his of deals would have instantly failed.
4. The man who owns a business has more to worry about than one who works for another.
5. Just as work must have a schedule, so must one's study and prayer.
6. Keeping oneself busy with work can save a person from sin.
7. Be thankful for the work you receive, for others may not even have this.
8. Always try to be a step ahead of your boss and the other employees. You will gain their trust and loyalty.
9. Do your work quickly and don't push it off. Then you will have time for the things you enjoy.
10. The Torah comes easily to one who desires it, and who makes his work secondary.
11. Always leave your work behind after you're finished for the day. There is no reason to mix work and family.
12. When you have faith that HaShem brings about your success with clients, HaShem brings you larger and more profitable ones.
13. Don't give too many chances to employees. You will probably end up disappointed time and again.

14. If you don't believe in your ability to succeed in business, how will you prosper?
15. Don't put all your funds into one investment.
16. There is no sure thing in business. If you think it's sure, you'll find out the hard way that it's not.
17. People will usually repeat the same financial mistakes a few times before they learn their lesson.
18. If you want to become wealthy, during your work connect to HaShem, with absolute faith and joy.

CHAPTER 30:
NIGHTLY SPIRITUAL PRACTICES

Written during a visit to Rabbi Akiva's grave during *chatzos*

1.   The first few minutes of *chatzos* are the most beneficial.
2.   Before reciting the *Tikkun (Tikkun Chatzos)*, praise HaShem (through your own words or by reciting Psalms 145-150), in order to be thankful and joyous in the holiness of this hour.
3.   Even to just think for a moment about the *Shechinah* and *Bais Hamikdosh*, at this hour of *chatzos*, is very great.
4.   A person can be attached to the *Shechinah* more after *chatzos*, than at any other hour of the day. This attachment is stronger with a *minyan* of men in study and prayer.
5.   Keep your *avodah* at this time as private as possible, between you and HaShem, as it is a time to grow in fear and humility.
6.   One can accomplish great things in the *mikvah* at this hour, more than immersion during the day.
7.   Every moment at this hour is more precious than pearls. Do not waste even a moment. It is like you're a top secret agent on an important assignment to protect the world.

Continued at Rav Chaim Luzzato's grave

8.   It is beneficial to go to a holy place and pray. If one goes *lishmah*, then all of the gates will open before him.

9. It is very important, when spiritually prepared, to learn the *sefer* Zohar Friday night after *chatzos*. This is the way of the sages.

10. Be warned: If you do not sanctify yourself at this holy hour of *chatzos*, and yet remain awake to waste time, swarms of impurities will look to draw from your spirit. Contrariwise, if you purify yourself, you could walk through fire unscathed; that is how holy your soul can become during this hour.

11. One can measure his level of fear of HaShem when going out in the night for *hisbodedus* (if it is safe in your area).

12. Talk to HaShem in *hisbodedus*, and you will not leave unanswered.

13. Even mundane activities and chores are elevated at this hour of *chatzos*

14. Waking up for *chatzos*, and then going to sleep before *netz*, is like preparing a gourmet meal and then leaving it out to spoil.

15. Too little sleep and too much sleep lead a person to sin, unless it is done for the sake of Heaven.

16. If you say *Tikkun Rochel* and *Leah* during *chatzos*, even abridged, your Torah study afterward will be *lishmah*.

17. Cry out at this time for your lack of knowledge and poor study habits. This is, after all, the time period of wisdom and understanding.

18. HaShem and the *tzaddikim*, are listening to your study and prayer at this hour. This means that you are spiritually surrounded by their holiness. Those who are wise know how to connect to this holiness, and will benefit from it in all ways.

CHAPTER 31:
PRAYER

1. Say the words of prayer with the intent of reaching the truth in your heart.
2. See the letters as worlds in and of themselves; expand them, draw them out, and they will shine for you.
3. When your prayer brings you to joy, know it has been accepted.
4. People think that by praying slowly their prayer is more devout, but often it can lead them to pride. Praying slowly can be good, but make sure it brings you to humility.
5. Make your prayers beautiful to HaShem with melody and tonality, and even the angels might join in.
6. To bring yourself to humility while praying, meditate on climbing the *sefiros* from *Malchut* to *Chessed*. Then picture any three-letter name in snow-like white, while flipping the order of the letters back and forth, until you reach complete humility and are like nothing (as taught by the Ramchal's students).
7. Prayer with energy and *d'vekus* will eventually lead to prayer with stillness, allowing only the soul to move. This is the *Chassidic* way of praying, but everyone usually prayers the opposite way.
8. Pacing back and forth and rocking arouses the heart.
9. Make set times and places to pray. Moving from this place even a few feet can change the prayer.
10. Accustom yourself to see *YKVK* and *Adna* intertwined, when reciting the holy name in prayer. During this time, have in mind the *kavanah* of elevating the *Shechinah*.

11. Every person can have *ruach hakodesh* while praying. They can see holy lights and have pure visions. Connect to the *Shechinah* and elevate Her, as is your purpose. Those who are wise will elevate Her many times over and over. Those even wiser will elevate all of Israel.

12. Absolutely, never say a word to anyone during prayer. This will cast out your soul from before the holy gates, making your prayer an abomination.

13. Reflect upon the great gift of prayer, and then pray happily.

14. When you pray with complete faith, your prayer reaches much further. Therefore, believe in the power of your prayer and HaShem's kindness.

15. There are many hidden reasons why particular names of HaShem are chosen for each prayer. Unfold these secrets, understanding them, and you will be like the Kings closest attendants with full access to His treasures.

16. Put yourself in every prayer, and identify with it in a personal way.

17. Pray for the needs of *Klal Yisrael* and the *Shechinah* during traditional prayer services. Then during *hisbobidus*, start by praying for yourself with the goal of eventually negating yourself and praying for all of Israel.

18. Prayer with the accompaniment of a *minyan* assures one entry, while praying alone, one can easily get lost.

CHAPTER 32:
PRAYER MEDITATIONS

1. Prayer said with little *kavanah,* but with concentration of the words, will eventually lead to prayer with true *kavanah.* During prayer, you should feel like your soul is almost going to expire from attachment in *d'vekus.*

2. Pray with all of your strength, shuckeling back and forth, at first, with great passion. Once you feel your soul going up towards the Heavens, remain completely still and pray softly.

3. It is wiser to pray for the *Shechinah,* and thereby include yourself inside the prayer in complete humility, than to pray only with yourself in mind. But there is a time for both ways.

4. Try to pray constantly in the same synagogue, and in the same seat, when possible.

5. If you understand the difference between the holiness and energy of each individual name of HaShem in the order of the prayers, you have the ability to change events happening in the world.

6. Imagine yourself while saying *amen* and *yehay shemay rabbah,* that you are in the lowest place of the world, completely humbled and small. Have in mind that you're attaching yourself to every Jewish soul in this world, and those in the Garden of Eden, that everyone should be elevated before HaShem.

7. People underestimate the power of the *chazaras hashatz* of the *Amidah,* by the prayer leader. They don't generally listen or follow inside the *siddur,* but instead think on other matters. Rather a person should meditate the entire time how the *Shechinah* is drawing down *shefa*

through the *chazzan*'s words. You can accomplish great things for the world in this way, if only you would appreciate *chazaras hashatz*.

8. Don't let the noises of others effect your concentration. Bear in mind that you are responsible for their souls. Concentrate on elevating this noisy and possibly confused person to higher levels of holiness, along with you. Prior to your attachment on high, you too were confused like him.

9. People think that praying slowly always means a higher concentration when sometimes, in fact, the reverse is true. Sometimes you're so attached to HaShem that the words come forth quickly and gracefully. There is then no need to dwell upon something already complete.

10. Attach yourself to each and every letter while you pronounce it. Consider from which of the five parts of your mouth the pronunciation is coming. Attach yourself to this sound, and its placement, through this you will connect to the root of each letter.

11. Imagine the letters on fire while you recite them, ascending to Heaven in smoke.

12. If you don't believe that HaShem hears your prayers, and don't even believe your own sincerity, how can the prayers be elevated?

13. Recite as many of the Psalms as you can daily, and learn them by heart, so you can recite them randomly throughout the day, thereby attaching yourself to HaShem.

14. It is good to know which *sefirah* you are addressing during each particular blessing of the *Shemonah Esrei*, so that you know what kindness you're trying to draw down from Heaven. This is done based on the different *nikudos* (as seen in some prayer books) of the letters that pertain to the *middos* of HaShem. The more familiar you are with this, the greater your ability to open the gates of prayer.

15. Asking people to pray for you is helpful as sometimes you need the assistance of another to get you out from a dark place.

16. Meditate on the compartments of your *tefillin*, and how each one represents a letter in HaShem's name *YKVK*.

17. Just as you pray with words, so too are you able to pray in thoughts, through meditating on *yichudim* and *psukim* in the Torah. Some *yichudim* and passages you can keep in your mind as you walk and go about your day.

18. Pray to HaShem, to improve your abilities and comprehension of prayer.

CHAPTER 33:
FEAR OF HASHEM

1. It is good to glance at the sky, in order to increase your fear of HaShem, but you can also glance at nature. At the trees, plants, mountains, and rivers. All of nature knows and fears its Creator.

2. Though it may be more productive, a hurried step can sometimes make one forget HaShem.

3. Spending time regularly with those who do not recognize HaShem can lead a person to forget Him. This would include watching broadcasts, listening to frivolous music and other such things on the media.

4. When you pray any passage that speaks about fear, concentrate more devoutly. Learn to feel what you say in your heart and bones, causing them to tremble from time to time, when thinking of the greatness of HaShem.

5. A person must learn the fear of HaShem, think about it and make it a part of them.

6. With fear of HaShem comes attachment to the *Shechinah*.

7. Clothing that covers oneself modestly instills fear of HaShem. This is especially so when worn for the sake of Heaven.

8. When you fear HaShem, those around you are affected positively. You're drawing them close to HaShem, even if they are very far. Don't underestimate this. Just standing in the street with true fear of HaShem can change the thoughts of those around you.

9. Look into the eyes of someone attached to HaShem and you will join him in holiness.

10. Your head should be slightly down and your eyes occasionally glancing upwards.

11. The grave of a *tzaddik* radiates fear of HaShem. It is a good place to acquire this important trait.

12. Walking in the holy land of Israel increases fear of HaShem.

13. Fear of HaShem brings a person to gladness.

14. If you don't think about fear of HaShem, you should force yourself to dwell on the topic; it will make you wise.

15. To fear HaShem is to know Him.

16. There is no end to the fear of HaShem, it is always like starting at the beginning because true fear of Hashem is endless.

17. If you don't fear HaShem this day, you haven't studied enough Torah *lishmah*. The Torah study done properly instills fear of HaShem and joy to one's bones.

18. If you hang around people who fear HaShem, they will draw this fear into you.

CHAPTER 34:
FRIENDSHIPS

1. Always greet a person (*shalom*, Hello…) first so they are the one to return the greeting.
2. A friend is someone who should be supportive and encouraging.
3. Friendships grow with openness and trust.
4. A friendship lasts when there is also an understanding of space.
5. Friendships that grow too quickly usually don't last.
6. Sometimes a potential friend is right before us, but we are too afraid to make the first connection.
7. People who appear to be happy attract friends, even if it is not a true happiness.
8. When telling over Torah to your friend, make sure it is at their level, and that it goes along with their character. In this way you will draw them closer to HaShem, otherwise, you might push they away.
9. A true friend takes the time to listen and doesn't just give advice. Listening should be the main thing.
10. Don't ask for too many favors of your friend, or you will eventually push they away.
11. If you can't be yourself with them, this person is not a true friend.
12. Always ask your friends how they are doing so that they can respond *baruch* HaShem, blessed be His Name.
13. A friend is someone who is there during the bad times, not just the good times.
14. A friend sees mostly the good in you, that is why they remain with you.

15. If your relationship doesn't draw you or them closer to HaShem, don't pursue it very often.

16. A person's greatest friend should be HaShem. He will never disappoint you, and His love is unending. Therefore, talk to Him often.

17. If you are drawn to something that isn't so good, keep your friends out of it. Meaning, do not allow them to stumble with you just so you won't go about making a mess alone. You can talk to them and ask for help, but you should never get them to join you in frivolous activities that can lead to sin.

18. If you're not a friend to yourself, how can you be for others?

CHAPTER 35:
WAKE UP

1. If you rise in the morning with positive thoughts, your day will be smooth and graceful. Therefore, switch your thoughts if you have to, but make sure to start your day with positivity.

2. Have in your thoughts the Divine name (*Aleph, Lamed, Vav, Hey*) *EloKah* when you start your day, as it is the garment for the soul.

3. Keep a wash basin next to your bed, and you will sleep better. This is a *segulah* for insomnia or bad dreams.

4. Say *Modeh Ani* every morning, with joy.

5. The less you talk before prayer, the less confused you will be during prayers, and the more acceptable they will be.

6. Do not involve yourself in too many activities before prayer. It is best to pray immediately after the *mikvah*.

7. Do not forget to say *birchas hatorah*, if you involve yourself in Torah activities before prayer.

8. Always glance at the morning sky. It draws down kindness and healing.

9. A wise person awakes before dawn and studies Torah, and then prays at sunrise.

10. How you start your day will decide how it finishes.

11. A high protein meal in the morning wakes a person up. A slice of bread makes a person strong.

12. Joy in the morning is important. How can you not be happy when you have another day to serve HaShem?

13. How you greet your family in the morning can ensure a day of peace.

14. Just as the entire world received sustenance from the practice of the *mamodos*, so too does it receive from the recital of the *karbonos*, in the beginning of your prayers. When you recite them, do so with sweetness and love, thereby removing judgment from Israel.
15. Think only positive thoughts and remove all traces of sadness.
16. When you wake up, make sure not to waste time. Rather, start your day ready to conquer the world.
17. Getting up early is a difficult habit to start, but its reward is endless.
18. If you allow yourself to be overwhelmed at the beginning of the day, the entire day will overcome you. Make sure to accept all obstacles with a smile and perseverance.

CHAPTER 36:
HAPPINESS

Written by the grave of Rav Korspedia

1. Your happiness should not be dependent on others.
2. A person accomplishes more when they are happy.
3. It is difficult to be happy when you're feeling fatigued.
4. When you are bombarded with excess thoughts, as a result of too much free time, your confusions can turn to depression.
5. A person is happy when they can give to others, thereby focusing less on themselves.
6. It is difficult to be happy when you owe money to others.
7. You have 613 reasons to be happy.
8. Procrastination turns matters of the past into unhappy, stressful situations.
9. A person satisfied with what they have, and doesn't think about what they lack, will always be happy.
10. When a person is content with their true self, and is not worried about looking good in the eyes of others, they are happy.
11. Singing a holy tune makes a happy heart.
12. It is good to express your unhappiness to a close friend or rabbi.
13. Unhappiness can come and go, but joy should be forever.

Written at Rav Tarfon's grave

14. Recital of *Tehillim* pushes away sadness.

15. Beautiful scenery eases the mind from sadness and anxiety.
16. Eating fruits helps a person to be joyous.
17. There are always reasons to be happy, find them and latch on.
18. Being sad is like allowing Satan the keys to the inner doors of your life. Why would you allow this?

CHAPTER 37:
HUMILITY / PRIDE

1. When a person is humble they can draw from *Chesed* and *Gevurah*, the right and the left sides simultaneously, thereby drawing down from Heaven both their spiritual and physical needs.
2. With humility comes divine inspiration.
3. Humility leads one to wisdom.
4. When a person attains humility during their prayers, it is a sign that their prayer is accepted.
5. The goal of all wisdom is to realize you are nothing. Through this high level of humility, you increase your wisdom and understanding.
6. The only way to truly be connected to HaShem is to think of yourself as nothing.
7. Ask yourself, "Who is the lowest Jew in the world?"
8. The *Shechinah* seeks out those who are humble and attaches to them.
9. People with pride draw to themselves friends who are just like them. Men full of falseness, leading an empty lifestyle.
10. A prideful person is never truly happy.
11. Pride pushes HaShem away.
12. People seek to learn from someone who has humility.
13. It is healthy to meditate on humility during prayer.
14. If there is one thing you should take pride in, it is that you are a Jew.
15. Singing with pure intentions can lead a person towards humility. If the intentions are for honor, they can lead one away from HaShem, and take those listening astray as well.

16. A humble person doesn't share everything they know.
17. One should be especially humble with their spouse.
18. You can see from the way a person eats if they are humble.

CHAPTER 38:
SHABBOS

1. The effort you put into *shabbos* is what you get out of it.
2. It is beneficial to light many candles for *shabbos*, especially with olive oil.
3. Try to personally cook at least one dish for *shabbos*, or to help prepare the food in some way.
4. A person should study as much Torah as possible on *shabbos*. *Sipurei Maysios* and spiritual teachings are especially beneficial.
5. Engaging in heartfelt singing on *shabbos* can bring a person to tremendous spiritual revelations.
6. The fish course on *shabbos* should be eaten slowly and with concentration. It is best to use your fingers, rather than a utensil, for the fish holds the soul of a *tzaddik*. The more concentration you have during this course, helps you to feel the elevation of the sparks in the holy *shabbos* fish.
7. Go out of your way as much as possible to have guests for *shabbos*. Of course, this should not be at the expense of your family.
8. It is good to go to the *mikvah*, *shabbos* morning, as early as possible. Everything can be attained through the *shabbos* morning *mikvah*. Connect yourself to many *tzaddikim* while immersing, as explained elsewhere.
9. Do not spare comfort on *shabbos*. Leave extra lights on so that the house is bright. Keep the thermostat at the most comfortable temperature, so as to spare no expense for the holy day.

10. What you talk about, and the way you talk, should be different on *shabbos*. Do not speak about things you are normally worried about or of weekly secular matters

11. When making *kiddush*, put around your *kiddush* cup 6 small cups filled with wine. The large cup represents the *shabbos*, and the 6 cups, the weekdays which draw their blessing from the *shabbos*.

12. Smell many spices before *shabbos* and during *shabbos* night.

13. Circle the *shabbos* table seven times, while reciting *Shalom Alechem*.

14. Those learning Zohar should do so especially on *shabbos* night after *chatzos*.

15. Make sure your hands are perfectly dry before making *hamotzee*, or touching anything, when washing for bread.

16. When reciting *kiddush*, have in mind the word גבילון, *gevilon* which is the secret of *shefa*, flowing from Heaven.

17. The *kiddush* cup represents all of the Jewish people. When you hand the cup from your left hand to your right, after it is raised by both, you are drawing holiness from the right to the left and thereby bringing blessing to all people. Continue to have the needs of *Klal Yisrael* in mind until the end of *kiddush*.

18. When you have your *seuda* for *shabbos*, a reflection of your table is above in the Garden of Eden. Therefore, concentrate that your *shabbos* table floating in the higher worlds.

CHAPTER 39:
ANGER

1. Just as fire destroys everything in its path, so does anger.
2. Once you overcome anger, you can easily destroy all other negative traits.
3. An angry person is really upset with HaShem, and this is a grave sin, similar to worshiping idols.
4. Anger blocks *shefa* and *parnasa* from coming down to you.
5. An angry person only hurts themselves, and makes their own situation worse.
6. Anger leads to depression.
7. One must never harbor anger at their children.
8. To rid yourself of anger, set aside a jar and drop a marble into it each time you feel angry. Let the action of dropping this marble take the place of being angry. Hear its sound and let your eyes see the marble drop, withdrawing the anger from within you.
9. Nobody likes a person who gets angry.
10. Learn to look for the good points in other people and in your life. This will cause you to be slow to anger.
11. What is the purpose of being angry when it really doesn't help you change the situation? The only way to improve circumstances is to accept them or plan a productive solution.
12. Anger stems from pride.
13. There is not enough room for HaShem in one's life if there is anger.
14. An angry person draws to himself many illnesses.

15. Someone who is angry at others is really angry with himself.

16. Speaking slowly and softly helps a person to change their natural tendency towards anger.

17. Never call out to anyone, even your children, in a loud voice. Speak calmly, and you will stay calm under all circumstances.

18. Anything you say to others, while angry, you usually will come to regret. So, keep silent! With *da'as*, release your troubled heart.

CHAPTER 40:
MUSIC

1. Music has the power to heal and the power to destroy.
2. When a person plays or sings music, this can fix all their flaws.
3. Composing songs is a small form of *ruach hakodesh*.
4. When you sing or play heartfelt songs the *malachim* join you. Sometimes it is without your notice.
5. Sometimes only music has the power to revive the soul.
6. The highest form of music is one that is no longer audible.
7. At first, let the words inspire you, then let the tune itself carry you even higher from level to level.
8. People hardly ever reach the real potential of a song because they end it too soon.
9. Let a song bring you into a meditative level.
10. A child who can sing beautifully can bring you to places nobody else can.
11. Everyone's taste in music is different. This shows how powerful it is, and how different our souls are.
12. There are times when only music can lift you up from a dark place.
13. It is good to hum a tune while studying Torah. It helps you remember your studies and connect your learning to high spiritual levels.
14. If you listen to a song enough times, you begin to enjoy it even if it's not really well written. This shows the power of the meditative side of melody.
15. It is good to learn to read musical notes. In the future world, the understanding of music can assist your enjoyment of the angels' songs.

16. If people are singing, make sure to join in, even in a hushed tone, as music sung with a group has the ability to lift everyone up together.

17. Listen carefully to the *tzaddik's* singing. Through him, you can attach yourself on high.

18. Each beat is another step on a spiritual ladder that you can climb. The secret of a bar of musical notes is to know how to ride it up to Heaven.

CHAPTER 41:
SPEECH

1. People underestimate the power of speech.
2. Speech has the power to give life or the power to destroy.
3. The *Shechinah* is drawn to someone who speaks in a soft tone, and withdraws from those using a loud strong voice.
4. Say what you need to and not more.
5. A wise person can connect any conversation to Torah thoughts, so much so that through simple dialogue they can elevate the world.
6. Talking too much can increase confusion, while talking a little can lessen your confusion. Sometimes it can even take a *taanis dibur* to regain focus.
7. If a person thought that they were being recorded, they would watch what they say carefully. The angels and HaShem are always surrounding us, and recording our words, in order to testify later, for and against us.
8. Be in the habit of not talking about others, even when it is not *loshon hara*, and then you will never come to err.
9. Better is the person who listens, than one who is always talking.
10. Talking in a positive way can turn even a bad situation into a good one.
11. Speaking without thinking hurts you spiritually, comparatively as eating rotten foods harms you physically.
12. A person can be in communication with others, while really being in connection with a world much higher.

13. If only we comprehended how much power our words contain. Ill speech can damage others, through speaking lightly without thinking first!

14. It can never be good to tease a person with words, even if they are accepting that it's only in jest.

15. A person can succeed in all relationships if he masters the art of speaking.

16. Speaking to a young child with love and sweetness is one of the most important things about *chinuch*.

17. Everything about a person is revealed through their tone of voice and the way they express what they want to communicate.

18. When you fix the way you talk to others, you are also purifying your heart.

CHAPTER 42:
ADVICE

1. A person should give advice only with kind words and selfless intentions.
2. It is easier for a person to take advice in a scenic, calm setting. This especially holds true near water.
3. A humble person's advice is taken seriously.
4. Giving advice at the wrong time can lead to more sins.
5. Most people give advice out of pride for themselves.
6. Don't give advice to someone while they are in the company of their friends.
7. During the evening, a person is more receptive to advice.
8. If you are not holding at the level of the advice you're giving, think twice before you give it.
9. The higher a person's purity, the more understanding they have about life.
10. Better to be silent than to question the advice of a *tzaddik*.
11. Even if the advice given to you, by a *tzaddik*, is wrong it can become correct, and carry with it a tremendous blessing.
12. Don't take advice from just anyone.
13. When you need advice, open up the *sefer* Ayin Yaakov to any page at random, and HaShem will lead you on a righteous path.
14. If you go to the grave of a *tzaddik* to pray, you will usually know what to do after.
15. Should you know that someone won't accept your advice, maybe it's a sign to leave him alone.
16. The best advice is given by example.

17. Sometimes the most important thing is not to give advice at all, but just to listen.
18. If you see many people are already advising someone, unless they are totally wrong, it is better to just show your friendly support instead of offering your opinion as well.
19. Don't give advice to someone wiser than you.

CHAPTER 43:
SPIRITUAL VISIONS

1. Spiritual awareness is something that grows as a person increases in holiness and purity. Also, practicing repetitive meditations on holy names opens many spiritual doors.

2. When a person has learned the spiritual experiences of sages like Ezekiel, their visions become more realistic and accurate.

3. One can see the most spirituality after immersing in the *mikvah*, or during intense Torah study.

4. A person can see better spiritually when in the presence of *tzaddikim*.

5. First, you have to rid yourself of your ego through singing and joy in HaShem, and only then are the Heavens open for you.

6. You cannot force spirituality. You need to invite it slowly, and then raise yourself up, step by step. Forceful attempts at spiritual revelations only fail.

7. Constant repetition and consistency are imperative for attaining spiritual visions.

8. Remove all doubt and connect to the holiness of your soul, in order to see visions revealed from the soul itself.

9. When you are connected to the *Shechinah*, you are constantly seeing visions, even though you may not be aware of it.

10. A person who sees things with selfish intentions, sees them with mistakes.

11. If it isn't *lishmah*, then don't enter the higher realms in your thoughts. You will find yourself becoming more confused.

12. One can attain the best revelations on *shabbos* and *yom tov*. The more effort you put into their preparation, the more you will receive in return.

13. If you are worthy, a holy person can connect to your mind, and share with you spiritual revelations even if you are unaware that its him purifying your soul.

14. Understanding music, and using it as a tool for the meditative process, is very helpful towards the attainment of spiritual visions.

15. Entering your thoughts into the spiritual, can draw negative attention from the evil husks. You should be properly prepared and seek a balanced Torah lifestyle.

16. Don't reveal all your spiritual revelations to others. Only those in which are already second nature to your soul, should you share.

17. You can accomplish great spiritual levels at the gravesite of a *tzaddik*, when you bind yourself to his soul.

18. Without joy and peace, your soul will be stuck in the world of *Asiyah*.

CHAPTER 44:
EATING

1. Your thoughts, while eating, can elevate you towards the path of righteousness or evil, depending on how the food is digested. Therefore, make sure to eat slowly and with concentration.
2. It is better to purchase food more often than to store up.
3. When you eat, make sure to concentrate on the blessing. What helps the most is to stop and think, "Let me say this blessing slowly with concentration."
4. Pray for your food and physical nourishment each day.
5. This is very important: Food has the power of *nogah* (a neutral level that can become holy or pure). When elevated with the proper intentions, food ascends out of *nogah*, returning the person and the sparks of holiness in the food to levels of purity. If a person doesn't eat with the right intentions, or if the food is not kosher to the highest standards, the person and the sparks inside the food fall, causing him to be faced with an inclination to sin.
6. Almost all sins stem from not eating properly. It is the main area in a person's life from where he draws power for good or evil.
7. Be careful not to eat while you are committing any improper act. This only emphasizes the power of the *klipah*.
8. It is very important to respect food. Many things we eat have holy sparks within them and can even be connected to Jewish souls of previous incarnations, awaiting rectification.

9. It is easy to remember to make a blessing before eating, but far easier to forget the one recited after. Therefore, make a sign for you to remember, maybe an object in front of you as a symbol, or a rubber band on your wrist.

10. Certain foods can warm or cool the body, effecting our emotions. They are also filled with vitamins and minerals. Therefore, it is important to balance the things we eat.

11. Depression causes a person not to eat and drink enough, or to overindulge in the wrong things. It is important to be aware of this and keep a balanced appetite, as weakness from a lack of good diet opens a person's heart to sin.

12. Before *bentching*, recite Psalm twenty-three; keep in mind that it is a *segulah* for wealth since the letters equal "*Zan*", which represents sustenance.

13. Food is elevated all the more when you prepare it yourself.

14. On weekdays, eating things you are allergic or intolerant to hurts a person physically and also spiritually. *Shabbos* can many times override this, in one or both aspects, since we are enhanced both spiritually and physically on this holy day.

15. Eat your food at the table, where it becomes like an offering in the Holy Temple.

16. To make your family members feel secure, always make sure there is plenty of food in the house.

17. Taking a moment before eating, to think about HaShem, is very helpful.

18. A person should be careful to eat well, and exercise regularly, so they can serve HaShem with strength.

CHAPTER 45:
CHILDREN

1. Children retain an unbelievable amount of information at a young age. Therefore, we should soak their minds each day with knowledge and faith.

2. When children speak we should listen. We learn this from HaShem, who listens to all His children's prayers.

3. The world would be a different place if parents would have listened, and given more attention to their children.

4. The Talmud says that the entire world is held up by the Torah study of children. We have to get involved in activities to help them.

5. We often blame the world's influences on effecting our children's perspective. But don't children simply mirror their parents?

6. Let's become a better example even behind closed doors. Children are so holy that they don't have to see us doing wrong, they just feel it.

7. We have to take upon ourselves the simplicity of being like a child with our Father in Heaven.

8. A child will do almost anything for a piece of candy and adults also enjoy rewards. HaShem has a storehouse filled with treats for adults. They simply need to follow His commandments.

9. You know why children don't have long attention spans? It is because their parents don't either.

10. A parent should always be one step ahead of their children.

11. A child's *rebbe* effects his life forever.

12. Most *chinuch* is learned at home. Parents are the main teachers for their children.
13. One of the most important things to teach a child is that they should perform the *mitzvos* wholeheartedly. This is mainly taught by a parent's joy, and purity of heart, while performing commandments in front of his kids.
14. If one's children are happy, their parent's *parnasa* increases tenfold. Teaching them to live with less and not spoiling them, will show them how to always be joyous later in life.
15. It is very important that children are taught to wash their hands and be clean.
16. The more toys a child has to play with, the less they learn to appreciate the things they already have.
17. If you want to connect to high spiritual levels, surround yourself with children.
18. If you can't appreciate children, what can you appreciate?
19. Cherish the holiness and simplicity of children. In their faces shines the light of a pure connection to HaShem.

CHAPTER 46:
DAILY PRACTICES

1.   It is good for everyone to take upon themselves to study a book that teaches about *emunah*, each day.

2.   A person should say daily, "*Shivisi* HaShem *lenegdi samid.* I have placed HaShem before me always."

3.   It is good to close one's eyes once in a while, and to think about fear of HaShem. When we close them we are able to connect more easily to spirituality.

4.   When conversing with others, we can also think about HaShem. If we hear mundane matters, we should think how they are really connected to HaShem and the Torah. This was the way of *tzaddikim* - to elevate the mundane to spirituality.

5.   It is good to leave small coins next to the charity box. This will remind you will place them inside more often, which will constantly make you think about HaShem.

6.   Kissing the *mezuzah* is often overlooked, as is walking respectfully in a backward motion when leaving the synagogue. Some people even walk up to the *bimah* to kiss the *aron* before leaving, to show respect to this holy place. Even if we don't feel anything from this, we are training ourselves to fear and love HaShem, by keeping these practices.

7.   It is good to wear our *tzitzis* outside of our clothing, to remind us of the *mitzvos*. This has value even if it only helps us subconsciously.

8.   One should glance at the sky every so often to increase his fear of HaShem, but also take a moment to enjoy its beauty. The glancing at the sky brings us the fear of

HaShem, while contemplating its beauty can give us the love of HaShem.

9. When we wash our hands, alternating three to four times on each hand, we remove the strength of the evil inclination. You cannot compare the renewed holiness by washing hands outside of the bathroom, to washing inside. For this reason, many sinks in Israel are made outside of the bathroom.

10. As much as we should be *bitul*, and think of ourselves as nothing, we must never forget and lose sight of our holiness. Every Jewish soul is constantly connected to a stream of holiness.

11. *Kashrus* enables one's soul to shine and to not be blocked by confusions. Our level of *kashrus* should always be improved upon and not static. There are very few people who keep all of the laws perfectly. A wise person is very careful when eating out. It really isn't okay to simply trust anyone in *kashrus* because of their scholarship. You would be surprised at the many mistakes being made in food preparation, by people who in other *mitzvos* are very careful.

12. Smiling is one of the greatest forms of *ahavas Yisrael*.

13. Positive energy is contagious. If you have been blessed with this aspect, you must share it. Even if you are not a positive person, with practice, you can be. A positive person can change their *mazal* for good.

14. With every deed, concentrate being completely inside the action so you can accomplish something wonderful within your heart as well.

15. Serve HaShem like a person employed by the King, with compassion, making His will first in your life.

16. Discipline yourself with your time management. You will become a productive and successful person.

17. You're not alone. HaShem is your best friend, and is always there for you. Don't be shy to bother Him at any time of the day with your problems, as He also desires your call.

18. Learn to care about others with all of your heart. The most important thing is to be a good and sincere person.

19. It is good to learn, or pray while standing, from time to time, to increase *d'vekus*.

20. In order to purify your eyes from glancing at unholy objects, open your eyes while immersing in the *mikvah*.

21. While wearing your *tefillin*, think about its four compartments, and how they correspond to the four letter name *YKVK*.

22. It is good to confess your sins to HaShem regularly, while visiting the grave of a *tzaddik*.

23. Always keep your body clean and without odor. Even more so, you should wear clothing that has been washed.

24. Cast a good eye on others, especially strangers, and thereby you can change their merit from bad to good.

25. Drinking liquids arouses a person to pray and sing songs.

26. Train yourself to appreciate the nature that surrounds you, and relate it to Torah passages. This will elevate you, and the living organisms back to HaShem.

27. Memorize many psalms by heart, so you can later recall them during your travels.

28. Overdress for most occasions in order to give extra respect to HaShem.

29. Think of yourself as holy, and eventually it will become a reality.

30. There is only one thing you should fake and that is to always appear happy to others. Eventually, it may become a reality, and at least you will make others smile in the meanwhile. If you are sad, though, don't sit by and wait. Find someone who can help you mend your broken heart.

31. Don't be afraid to buy the things you truly need, when you are lacking them. HaShem will refill your pockets through your faith.

32. Imagine yourself alone in the desert, and call out to HaShem in simplicity and humility.
33. Stop yourself from being extreme. It is important to live life with balance.
34. If you are worrying, you are not living.

CHAPTER 47:
CALMING PASSIONS

1. The more you feed your passions, the stronger they become.
2. If a person would just wait a few minutes, a few hours, maybe even a few days, before following their urges, they would slowly dissipate on their own.
3. Decisions made out of passion or love don't always work out the way you expected.
4. Should you not be able to control your thoughts, simply switch them to another direction, and eventually they will go away. This is because a person can have only one clear thought at a time.
5. Trying to control one's passions, without Torah study, is like trying to put out a fire without any water.
6. Say *Shema* with concentration, and it will help at that moment to subdue your desires.
7. People run after passions, sometimes just out of habit, because the sin has become second nature. These are the most difficult sins to get rid of, and the only remedies are increased Torah study, *mikvah*, keeping yourself busy with other things and retraining your good actions to be by rote.
8. The *tzaddik* is able to help calm your passions, but you must be willing to lower your pride to speak with them about it.
9. Often people crave things that are not good for them because their imagination lacks holiness, and the knowledge of what is truly important - a healthy soul and body.

10. Elevate your passions by finding some comparable *middah* in HaShem that you can think about instead.
11. When you feel a strong desire for something physical, teach yourself to wait, and take a step back, to evaluate if it's truly important.
12. There is nothing greater than a true passion for Torah and *mitzvos*.
13. Learn to become a balanced person so you never act completely on emotion.
14. Passions change over time leading you find new items to desire.
15. Ask a friend if your desire is practical or not.
16. Passion can overwhelm the mind so much that you forget the Torah and HaShem.
17. If you're happy, you are able to control your passions and desires.
18. Think about the *sefirah* of *Chesed,* and direct your thoughts there. This elevates the passions of love away from the mundane, back to their source in holiness.

CHAPTER 48:
SPREADING KINDNESS

1. If people showed more kindness and respect for one another, the redemption would have taken place immediately.
2. Some people find it easy to spread their kindness among relatives or like-minded people. The real test is to spread kindness to others who are different.
3. People who look upon others with a good eye are doing a great favor to them..
4. When you are kind to others, you feel good and complete inside.
5. Giving your energy to another helps take your mind off your own problems.
6. The more you give of yourself to others, the more you share in the *middos* of HaShem, and unite with Him.
7. Kindness to another is everlasting.
8. As long as you have your basic needs taken care of, it is more important to give to others than to yourself.
9. Sweet and caring words have the ability to give life to another person.
10. Most people need help but are too embarrassed to ask for it.
11. Don't wait for someone to ask for assistance. Look for the opportunity and volunteer.
12. A person is sometimes stuck in the loop of life's pressures, and only a kind-hearted person can get them out.
13. Giving money to another person is a great kindness, and HaShem will always return the favor.

14. We learn to be kind to others from HaShem. If you appreciate the kindness HaShem does for you, you will seek methods to follow in His footsteps.
15. Sometimes taking care of yourself is also a kindness, to those who depend on you.
16. Your family always needs more love and compassion. Increase the quality of time you spend with them and the kind deeds you do for them. Sometimes they feel ignored and hurt that they are neglected, while you do kindness for others.
17. There are some people who simply don't know how to be nice to others. Others carry around so much pain that they act on survival mode, and can't see outside themselves. Inside might be a beautiful soul that only needs a kindness in order to sprout.
18. The people receiving your kindly act can tell if it's heartfelt or not. Therefore, if you want to do an act of *chesed*, do it with all your heart.

CHAPTER 49:
MOSHIACH

1.   Jews don't have to have perfect peace amongst them. The *moshiach* will come as soon as people at least try to care about getting along with one another, but this simple step seems a huge mountain to overcome.

2.   Can you imagine that you're in a marathon and thousands of people are waiting for you to reach the finish line, but you're running the wrong way or leisurely enjoying breaks along the way? Our relatives are watching above, wondering why we don't repent and do more *mitzvos*.

3.   If people really wanted the *moshiach* to come, he would be here.

4.   Don't you want to leave this world knowing you did everything you could to usher in the redemption for your descendants?

5.   All of us worry about our children and care for them with all our hearts, but we should provide our families not only with material life insurance but also an everlasting one that will hasten the *moshiach* even after we leave this world.

6.   If only people realized the power that even one Jewish soul has to bring the final redemption! There is no such thing as just an ordinary Jewish soul.

7.   The *moshiach's* arrival is more imminent than we realize because we can feel him so close, the last waiting period feels like forever.

8.   Hasten the *moshiach's* arrival with an increase in the performance of good deeds for others.

9. Through studying about the messianic times, you become part of the redemption itself.
10. Torah study with the intention of true change and actual practice is what draws the *moshiach* closer.
11. A person of true faith has to believe in the *moshiach*.
12. As my father zt"l used to say, "Does it matter if the *moshiach* comes on a Friday or a *shabbos*?" If he comes first from the north or the south? Let him just come anywhere and anytime.
13. Like most things in *Yiddishkeit*, it is best to take the middle path when it comes to the *moshiach*. Believe in his imminent arrival, prepare yourself with the learning of *karbonos* and the laws of messianic times, yet try to give over messianic teachings to others gently, without force.
14. Telling over stories and Torah teachings from the messianic times inspire a person to have faith.
15. If you want to bring the *moshiach*, remove all hate from your heart.
16. The study of Torah at midnight and the recital of *tikkun chatzos* are the best *tikunim* a person can do to usher in the messianic times.
17. If someone you know is reciting *tikkun chatzos* and studying Torah at midnight, know that this person has a portion in the final redemption. Do everything you can to help him. Even if it means through charity, picking up his kids at daycare or bringing him meals.
18. Those who arise for *chatzos* to do *avodas* HaShem have a special power to bless others, as they are connected to the roots of *shefa* and the *moshiach* himself.

CHAPTER 50
SHIDDUCHIM

1. HaShem is constantly making matches to keep the world, and all events, turning.
2. A person should be practical in what match might fit them because HaShem isn't going to bring your *bashert* to you when you're not ready to accept them.
3. You need to make ordinary *histadlus*, and nothing more, to find your *bashert* because the time and place comes completely from HaShem.
4. Personal hygiene and cleanliness is important preparation for a *shidduch*.
5. Being a balanced person helps to find one's rightful match.
6. A person has to reach a level of *bitul*, and be willing to give of himself in order to share his life with another human being.
7. Finding good friends, who encourage you in serving HaShem, is similar to finding a *shidduch*.
8. It is important to avoid the wrong friends because, if your friends are attached to sin, they will drag you to this dark place with them.
9. Ask the *tzaddik* to pray for you that you find the right match easily. He too is involved in keeping the world going and making sure people's spiritual needs are met.
10. Matchmakers are good, but many *shidduchim* can end up through the intermediary of close friends.
11. The right *shidduch* usually comes when you least expect it.

12.   You can't really push a *shidduch* before its right time. Therefore, the best thing is to relax and stay busy, so as not to get lost during your hunt for companionship.

13.   The most important thing about a partnership is that you have similar goals and ideals.

14.   Looks and fashion can be distracting when trying to find a match with a kind-hearted person. Appearances are only temporary, so don't get caught up on physical beauty which is not everlasting.

15.   Sometimes the beauty of a person grows on you as they mature and gain self-confidence. Therefore, don't be so quick to judge.

16.   The best way to bring your *shidduch* closer is to put your entire mind and heart into the study of Torah. Through the holiness of your study and self-growth, the *shidduch* will come on its own.

17.   Every match brings you closer to your destined *bashert*.

18.   The purer your thoughts, heart, and body, the sooner you are ready for your match. This applies not only to a *shidduch* but also to a business partnership, *chavrusa*, purchase of a home and all events in your life.

GLOSSARY

ARON - Chest. The cabinet where the Torah scrolls are kept

AVODAH - Service

BAIS HAMIKDOSH – The Holy Temple

BAIS MEDRASH - Jewish study hall located in a synagogue, yeshiva, kollel or other building

BENTCHING – Blessing after eating bread

BINAH - Understanding

BIRCHAS HATORAH – Blessing recited over the gift of Torah Study

BITUL - Nullified or selfless

CHATZOS - Midday or Midnight

CHAVRUSA – Study Partner

CHAZARAS HASHATZ – Repetition of the Amidah prayer by the Chazan

CHESED – Kindness, One of the Ten Sefirot

CHINUCH – Teaching Children

CHOCHMAH - Wisdom

CHOL HAMOED - (lit. "Weekday during the festival"); the semi-festive intermediate days of Passover and Sukkos

DAAS - (lit. "Knowledge"); the third of the Ten Sefiros, or Divine Emanations

DEVEKUS - Referring to closeness to G-d

EMES – Truth

EMUNAH - Faith

ERETZ YISRAEL - Israel

FEAR OF HASHEM – Fearing G-d

GASHMIUS - Materialism

GEVURAH – Severity, One of the Ten Sefirot

HALACHIC - Jewish Law

HAMOTZEE – Blessing over bread

HISBODIDUS – Meditation in the form of talking to Hashem

KARBONOS – Sacrifices

KASHRUS - Jewish dietary laws

KAVANAH - Concentration, intent. The frame of mind required for prayer or performance of a mitzvah (commandment)

KEDUSHA - Holiness

KLAL YISRAEL - The Jewish people

LISHMAH- The performance of the commandments for the sake of the mitzvah itself without ulterior motives.

LOSHON HARA – Negative talk about another person

MALACHIM - Angels

MALCHUS - Kingship

MEZUZOS – (lit. Doorposts) A case attached to the doorposts of houses, containing a scroll with passages of scripture written on it

MIDA /MIDDOS – Character trait(s)

MIKVAH - Ritual bath house

MINYON - The quorum necessary to recite certain prayers, consisting of ten adult Jewish men

MODEH ANI – Morning prayer to say when awakening

MUSSAR - contemplative practices and exercises for character correction

NETZ - Praying at the exact time of listed sunrise

NIGUNIM - Song

NEKUDOS - Vowels

OHOM HABAH – (lit. The World to Come) 1) The messianic age 2) the spiritual world that souls go to after death.

PARNASA - Income or livelihood

PESUKAY DEZIMRA - Psalms recited at the beginning of the daily prayer.

PIDYON - Redemption given to a sage to pray for you

POSUKIM - Verses

RACHMANUS - Compassion

RAV – Rabbi who answers Questions

RUACH HAKODESH - Divine Inspiration
SEFARIM - Books
SEFIRAH – Emanations
SEGULAH - A protective or benevolent charm or ritual
SHALOM BAYIS – Peace between husband and wife
SHECHINAH - The Divine Presence
SHEFA – Blessing from Heaven
SHEMONEH ESREH - Eighteen prayers said three times daily as part of the service
SHIDDUCH - Match
SIMCHAS - Joy
TANACH - Acronym of Torah (Law), Nevi'im (Prophets) and Ketuvim (Writings). Written Torah
TANIS DIBUR – A Fast from Talking
TEFILLIN - Holy Scriptures wrapped in a box with leather straps to attach to the head and arm
TEHILLIM - Psalms
TIKKUN - Repair
TIKKUN CHATZOS - (lit. "Midnight service"); a prayer recited by pious Jews at midnight, lamenting the destruction of the Holy Temple
TIKKUN HABRIS – Purity of the Covenant
TIKKUN HAKLALI – 10 Psalms recited as a General Remedy for all problems, especially to enhance sexual purity (Remedy discovered by Rebbe Nachman of Breslov)
TIKUN - Rectification
TZADDIK / TZADDIKIM - Righteous Persons
TZITZIS – A four cornered garment with strings attached to each corner
YEHAY SHEMAY RABBAH - Short response of the congregation to Kaddish
YETZER HARA - Evil inclination
YETZER HATOV – (lit. Good impulse) The moral conscience which motivates us to follow G-d's law
YICHUDIM - Unifications
YIDDISHKEIT - (Yiddish) Torah-Judaism
YIRAS HASHEM -Fear of God

YOM TOV (YOMIM TOVIM) - (lit. "Good day") A Jewish holiday

Sefer Yom-Leyom

Made in the USA
Columbia, SC
14 September 2018